Scribbles And Random Truths

By- Daneet Kaur

"Born to run, but who set the track?"

Published by Daneet Kaur
ISBN: **978-93-343-0599-9**

Disclaimer:
This book is intended for informational and inspirational purposes only. It is not a substitute for professional medical, psychological, or legal advice. If you are struggling with mental health challenges, please seek support from a licensed professional. The author and publisher are not responsible for any outcomes resulting from the use of this book.

Cover design by
First Edition
Printed in India

INDEX

INTRODUCTION

So, When Exactly Were They Gonna Explain Life?

Remember when we were kids and thought grown-ups had everything figured out? Like, they just *knew* how to do taxes, parallel park, and keep plants alive? Turns out, they were just winging it. And now, here we are—supposedly "grown-up" but mostly just *googling everything and hoping for the best.*

This book isn't going to give you a 10-step plan to success, or tell you to wake up at 5 AM and drink kale smoothies for ultimate productivity. Nope. This is more like one of those **late-night convos with a friend**, where you sit on the floor, question all your life choices, and realize—wait, *is everyone just faking it?* (Spoiler: Yes.)

No preaching, no sugarcoating—just the raw, funny, occasionally messy truth about growing up in a world that expects us to have everything figured out.

At some point, we were all told that life would follow a script. Get good grades, go to college, land a stable job, buy a house, and live happily ever after. But what they forgot to mention is that this script was *written by someone who had no idea what Wi-Fi was.*

And let's be honest—most of us have already broken some of the "rules." We were supposed to be financially responsible by 18, but here we are, spending half our pay check on overpriced coffee and *mysteriously losing socks in the wash.* We were told that love, success, and happiness would all come easily if we just followed the plan. Instead, we've got dating apps, career confusion, and an unhealthy attachment to fictional characters.

If you've ever felt lost, overwhelmed, or like everyone else got a *how-to-adult* guidebook except you—congrats, you're normal. And you're in the right place.

Now, let's get into the mess.

CHAPTER-1

Chapter 1: So, What Do You Wanna Be When You Grow Up? ...Uh, Alive?

"What do you wanna be when you grow up?"

As kids, this was an innocent question. The kind adults asked while ruffling our hair, expecting answers like astronaut, doctor, or fairy princess. (Side note: Why was 'princess' a *career* option? Like, where was that job application?)

But at some point, this harmless question morphed into something *terrifying*. It stopped being about dreams and became an interrogation about our *entire existence*. And suddenly, answering *"I don't know"* wasn't cute anymore—it was *concerning*.

See, the problem is that we were raised on the myth that people *just know* what they're meant to do. Like some divine voice whispers in your ear at 16: *"Congratulations, you are now destined to be an engineer. Here is your calculator and a slight caffeine addiction. Good luck."* But in reality? Most of us are just **guessing**.

Remember when every future job we imagined came with a cool uniform? Astronauts got space suits. Doctors got white coats. Firefighters had those epic helmets. Even chefs had those giant, ridiculous hats that made them look like they were hiding a whole loaf of bread under there. Life was simple—pick a career, get a costume, live your dream.

And then we grew up, and reality hit like a poorly aimed frisbee to the face. Turns out, most jobs don't come with cool outfits (unless you count the existential crisis hoodie we wear while contemplating life at 2 AM). Nobody hands you a crown for surviving adulthood, and no one announces, "Congrats, you are now a successful grown-up!"—which, honestly, feels like a design flaw.

And speaking of flawed designs—remember when we thought we'd have our lives together by, like, 21? Yeah. That was adorable. As kids, 21 sounded ancient. Like, full-blown mortgage-and-life-wisdom territory. Meanwhile, actual 21-year-olds are out here googling "how to do taxes" and eating cereal for dinner. Not exactly the mature, responsible adults we imagined. But here's the thing—back then, nobody cared if we changed our minds every five minutes. One day, you were an astronaut. The next, you were a detective solving *The Case of Who Ate the Last Cookie* (spoiler: it was you). No one told us we were failing because we couldn't stick to one thing. We were just *exploring*. So why does that suddenly stop when we grow up?

I spent my middle school years at Vivek High School, convinced I was going to crack UPSC and become some power-packed bureaucrat. (Spoiler: That didn't happen.) But even before that, since Class 3, creative writing had my heart. I didn't know what I'd do with it, but I knew I loved it. And I wasn't alone in that journey.

The school itself was *massive*—long corridors that felt like they stretched into another dimension, classrooms filled with a mix of the best people you'd ever meet and the ones who'd make you rethink your will to exist. (Yes, I'm talking about that one kid who never let anyone borrow a pen.) The teachers? A delightful spectrum. Some were legendary, some terrifying, and some could crack jokes better than a Netflix special.

And then, of course, there was the *running*. Oh, the running. Running to class because the bell rang while you were still stuffing chips in your mouth. Running away from the class prefect because you were *definitely* supposed to be in your seat. Running to the canteen to beat the lunchtime rush. Life was basically a marathon, but with fewer medals and more last-minute homework panics.

Despite the chaos, I had a great friend group. We weren't exactly the "future CEOs" of the school, but we had a blast. I wasn't even worried about *what* I'd do in life back then—I was too busy sneaking into the library, escaping into the world of books and novels, avoiding reality like a pro. (Honestly, if avoiding responsibilities was an Olympic sport, I'd have at least two gold medals.)

Enter Neeraj Ma'am, my Class 6 and 7 teacher—the kind of teacher who didn't just teach subjects but nurtured dreams. She had this sixth sense for spotting potential, like some kind of literary talent detector. To 11-year-old me, writing was just a fun thing I did, like collecting random stickers or believing I could train my dog to understand full sentences. But Neeraj Ma'am? She saw something more. She hyped up my words like they belonged in a Pulitzer-winning novel, even when they were basically just dramatic diary entries disguised as essays. She created a space where I wasn't afraid to express myself, where even my most cringeworthy metaphors were met with a gentle "Hmm, interesting choice" instead of straight-up laughter. She didn't just mark my work; she made me believe that my voice mattered.

And then came the career counselling sessions in Class 10—the moment where they sat us down, looked into our bright, slightly confused teenage eyes, and basically said, "So, what are you gonna do for the next 50 years?" (No pressure.) According to them, I was an obvious fit for commerce or humanities (with math, of course, because why not add suffering to creativity?). But plot twist—I took science instead. *Biggest mistake of my life(just kidding, these two years were fun)* Or at least, it felt like it at first. I spent half of Class 11 regretting my choices, wondering why I voluntarily chose to suffer. But now, as a Class 12 student, I can *almost* say I love math. Almost. (Let's not get carried away.)

There was one person in school who somehow knew exactly when I needed a sarcastic comment to survive a busy day in school 'Y'. Y had this eerie talent for sensing when I was on the verge of either having an existential crisis or throwing my physics book out the window. It was like they had a built-in radar for my academic and emotional meltdowns.

When the pressure was suffocating, when my brain felt like a malfunctioning Google search tab with 57 questions open at once, Y always had something to say—sometimes helpful, sometimes just ridiculously stupid, but always *perfectly timed.*

They weren't the type to help me decipher calculus or explain why my experiment results looked like they came from another dimension. But when life felt overwhelming—when the pressure, the expectations, and the never-ending mental to-do list got too much—Y just *knew.* A well-timed joke, a casual 'you're overthinking again,' or just the simple fact that they were *there* made all the difference. And for that, I'm still grateful."

Oh, and remember how everyone said, "After Class 10, you'll finally enjoy your life"? Yeah, that was a scam. A straight-up lie. Life didn't magically transform into some teenage dream sequence. If anything, it got more hectic. Turns out, life doesn't pause for you to *finally* have your main character moment. It just keeps going at full speed until you're old, sitting in a rocking chair with grandkids, wondering how the hell time flew by so fast.

Oh, but let's not forget—I was in the *student council.* Ah, yes, the prestigious title that made me feel like I had conquered the world… until I realized it also came with stress levels high enough to rival my pre-board anxiety. I was the *Protocol Captain (Girls)*—which sounded all fancy and powerful, but in reality, it mostly meant running around ensuring discipline while also pretending I had everything under control. (Spoiler: I did not.)

At first, I was ecstatic—ready to be a responsible leader, make a difference, and totally *not* just enjoy the clout that came with it. But soon enough, I realized that the 'council' part of the student council basically meant running around like a headless chicken while attempting to maintain an illusion of authority. Because let's be honest, telling other students to behave when I myself was seconds away from losing my sanity? Ironic.

And leading this whole operation? *Ira Bedi Ma'am.* Our maths teacher, our student council in-charge, and quite possibly the only person who could make both calculus and discipline sound terrifyingly important. She had this *way* of keeping us on our toes—her favorite line being, *"Be on your duty areas."* (As if any of us dared to be anywhere else when she was around.)

But the *real* fear factor? The casual way she'd mention that she went for board paper checking. *Board. Paper. Checking.* Every time she dropped that little fact in class, we'd collectively freeze. Because if *she* was checking papers, that meant somewhere out there, a poor student was staring at their answer sheet wondering why their perfectly fine step-by-step solution was now a big, fat zero. (Okay, maybe she wasn't *that* strict, but the fear was real.)

And then, of course, there was her *iconic* dialogue, one that's basically burned into our memories: *"When I went to St. Stephen's, every child was so well-dressed and well-behaved. I don't know why this school's kids act the other way."* Every time she said it, we'd exchange glances like, *Well, ma'am, we don't know either. Maybe it's the Punjab air. Maybe it's just… us.*

But for all the stress, all the lectures, and all the *mildly terrifying* board paper-checking stories, she was honestly one of the sweetest teachers we had. She cared, she taught with patience, and most importantly—she made sure we were scared *just* enough to do our work.

And then there's **Kabir**, my little brother, a certified member of the **"I'll Be Everything When I Grow Up"** club. Some days, he's dead serious about becoming an astronaut—until he realizes space has no WiFi. Other times, he's a detective, solving imaginary mysteries with an intensity that could put Sherlock to shame (even though his biggest clue is usually a half-eaten biscuit). And currently, Kabir has entered his **businessman era.** His grand plan? A **chocolate empire.** He's convinced that selling chocolates will make him **richer than Elon Musk**, and honestly, the confidence is admirable. Every day, he pitches new ideas—chocolates that never melt, chocolates with secret toys inside, chocolates that **somehow** make you taller (I suspect he's making this one for himself). He even tried selling me my own Dairy Milk, claiming it had "sentimental value" and was now worth double. **Entrepreneurial spirit or daylight robbery? Jury's still out.**

But that's Kabir—dreaming fearlessly, scheming endlessly, and **never doubting for a second** that he's meant to take over the world. But that's the beauty of it, isn't it? He **doesn't** have to pick one thing yet. He wakes up every morning with a brand-new dream and **zero fear of failure**—because to him, everything is still possible. No overthinking, no self-doubt, just pure **kid energy**. And watching him, I sometimes wonder… **when did we stop believing we could be anything?**

And this is the same Kabir who, after every exam, walks out like he just aced the UPSC. "How was it?" we ask. "Wonderful!" he beams, as if he just wrote a best-selling novel instead of a test. But the real fun begins when we ask, **"What questions came?"** Without fail, **every single time**, he gives us a blank stare, blinks a few times, and says, **"Uhh… I don't remember." Not a single question.** As if the moment he stepped out of the exam hall, the paper self-destructed in his brain. It's a mystery how he writes full answers but cannot recall a single word two minutes later. Maybe that's his secret to staying stress-free—**out of sight, out of memory.** If only I could master that level of selective amnesia.

But if there's one thing Kabir **does remember**, it's how much he **hates learning computer science theory.** He loves computers—loves playing games, clicking random buttons, and pretending he's hacking into top-secret government files. But the moment the textbook opens and words like

"algorithm" and **"binary"** appear, his soul visibly leaves his body. "Why do I need to know this? I just want to play Minecraft," he groans. I told him even businessmen need computers. He countered that **he'll just hire an IT guy.** Honestly? Can't argue with that logic.

The Pressure to Have It All Figured Out

At 18, you're supposed to decide a career. At 22, you're supposed to land the *perfect* job. By 30, you should have a house, a stable income, and a dog (because apparently, adulthood = dog ownership). But... who made these rules? And why does it feel like a speedrun?

Truth bomb: *Most adults are still figuring it out.* The ones who seem like they've got it together? Half of them is internally screaming. The other half are faking confidence so well, they've even convinced themselves.

And while we're at it—why did we think adults had all the answers? These were the same people who told us we couldn't swim for an hour after eating *or else we'd die.* Turns out, that was a lie. And yet, we still act like they *totally* knew what they were talking about when they said, "You need to have a solid career plan by 18."

Let's be real: if we still change our Starbucks order every week, how are we supposed to commit to a *lifelong* career choice? Imagine if 7-year-old you had to pick their forever job. Half of us would be professional dinosaur hunters. Some of us would be full-time mermaids. One or two ambitious souls would be both.

And yet, we still act like there's a *right* answer. If you don't have a grand career plan by 21, you're doomed to a life of failure and eating instant noodles forever. Not that instant noodles are bad. (Honestly, they're a lifestyle.)

Breaking the Myth of the 'Perfect Plan'

There's this idea that if you don't have your life sorted by a certain age, you've failed. But guess what? *Life doesn't work like that.* Some people find their passion at 12. Some stumble into it at 35. Some try one thing, hate it, and start over. And that's *normal.*

Take me, for example. As a kid, I thought I'd be a pilot. Then an IAS officer. Then an IPS officer (because apparently, I was ambitious *and* dramatic). I even had a phase where I was convinced, I'd become a scientist—until I realized that science involves *math*, and well, that was the end of that dream. The point is, I had no idea. And honestly? I still don't have a *final* answer. But that's okay.

At some point, we've all had our share of "I'm totally going to be this!" moments. One day, it's marine biologist (thanks, Shark Week). The next, it's lawyer (thanks, Suits). Then you hit an existential crisis when you realize you don't even *like* arguing or deep-sea creatures that much. The cycle repeats.

So, if you're currently panicking about the future, take a breath. The truth is, there's no universal deadline for success. No magical age where everything suddenly makes sense. The only thing you *have* to do is keep going, keep trying, and figure it out at your own pace.

Because at the end of the day, success isn't about sticking to a plan—it's about finding what actually makes you happy.

But What If I Choose Wrong?

Ah, the biggest fear of all: *What if I waste years on something, only to realize it's not for me?* First of all, welcome to being human. Second, *nothing is wasted* if it teaches you something about yourself.

Steve Jobs dropped out of college and took a random calligraphy class. That class? It led to the typography you see on Apple products today. J.K. Rowling's first book got rejected 12 times before Harry Potter became a cultural phenomenon. Oprah was told she wasn't fit for television.

Imagine if they had all given up because their first plan didn't work out?

Every experience—whether it feels like a detour, a mistake, or a failure—adds up to something. Maybe it's a new skill, a new perspective, or just the realization that you *never* want to do that thing again. Either way, you're moving forward.

The Secret No One Tells You

The truth? Most of the people who look like they've got life figured out are *faking it*. Even the ones with fancy LinkedIn bios and job titles that sound important. Even the adults who told us we had to have a plan. Even the ones who *seem* successful but are secretly wondering if they took the wrong path.

And that's freeing, isn't it? It means we can take our time. We can change our minds. We can try, fail, and try again. Because at the end of the day, there's no perfect plan—there's just *your* journey.

And sure, society loves to tell us that if we don't have our dream job, a stable income, and a pet dog by 30, we've failed. But who *made* these rules? And more importantly, why do they assume I want a dog? Maybe I want a raccoon. Maybe I want *no* pets and just a thriving collection of houseplants that are 50/50 on whether they'll survive the week.

Because if you think about it, we **never stop changing.** Our **favorite food changes.** Our **music taste changes.** (Remember when we thought the cringiest songs were masterpieces? Yeah, let's not talk about it.) Even the way we see the world shifts as we go through different phases of life. So why wouldn't our **dreams and ambitions evolve, too?**

And that's the secret no one tells you: **you are allowed to change your mind.** Not once. Not twice. **As many times as you need to.**

The truth is, life is messy. People change. Careers evolve. And sometimes, you think you've got it all figured out, only to realize three years in that you *actually* hate what you're doing (see: every mid-twenties identity crisis ever). And that's fine. We weren't *meant* to have all the answers at 18. Or 21. Or 30. Or maybe ever.

"Final Verdict: We're All Just Making It Up"

So, here's where we land: **no one really knows what they're doing.** Some people just have better LinkedIn bios.

And that's actually **a relief.** It means we don't have to have it all figured out. We don't need to stick to one dream like it's a legally binding contract. We don't have to panic every time we feel lost because—guess what? **So is everyone else.** Even the ones who look like they've got their life together. Even the ones who post aesthetic morning routines with motivational captions. Even the ones who confidently say, "I always knew I wanted to be a [insert fancy job title here]." (Did you, though? **Did you really?**)

So the next time someone asks, **"What do you want to be when you grow up?"**—whether you're 8, 18, or **pushing 40 with an existential crisis**—feel free to answer with:

> "Still deciding."
> "A work in progress."
> "Someone who hopefully gets eight hours of sleep someday."

Because here's the thing—**changing your mind isn't failure.** It's growth. It's realizing that maybe the dream you had when you were 10 doesn't fit the person you are now, and that's okay. It's understanding that life isn't meant to be one straight road with clear signposts. It's more like a **chaotic GPS system** that reroutes every time you discover something new about yourself.

Some people take a direct route and land where they always wanted to be. Others take detours, make U-turns, and discover places they never even knew existed. And sometimes, the best destinations are the ones you **never planned for.**

So if you're worried about "figuring it all out," here's my advice: **don't.** Instead, focus on **figuring yourself out.** Explore, experiment, mess up, try again. And trust that even if you don't have all the answers right now, you'll get there—**wherever 'there' may be.**

And if that doesn't happen? Well, **there's always the chocolate business.** (Kabir, I'm looking at you).

CHAPTER 2

Chapter 2: "Congratulations, You're a Disappointment!"

(Because no matter what you do, someone's always unimpressed.)

Remember when you were five, and people clapped because you counted to ten? No, seriously—*counted to ten.* You could've skipped a number, said them out of order, and your parents still would've acted like you just split the atom. Life was *good.* You got gold stars for existing, applause for remembering your ABCs, and a standing ovation if you managed to eat your veggies without a meltdown.

Fast forward a decade, and suddenly, things aren't so cute anymore. You solve equations that look like ancient spells, write essays that could make Shakespeare break into a sweat, and memorize enough chemical reactions to qualify as a part-time scientist. And what do you get? A disappointed sigh because you missed *two marks* in math. Two marks. Back in kindergarten, two marks would've been the difference between a random scribble and a masterpiece worthy of fridge display. Now? It's apparently the difference between "Wow, you're so smart!" and "You should've tried harder."

Welcome to your teenage years—where nothing is ever *quite* enough. You could cure a disease, save a cat from a burning building, and still hear, "That's nice, but did you do your homework?" No matter how hard you try, there's always *something* missing. Got a 98%? "Why not 100?" Helped around the house? "That's your responsibility." Won an award? "Well, what's next?" You could single-handedly bring world peace, and someone would still ask why you haven't started preparing for next semester's exams.

And the worst part? You start believing it. You start thinking that maybe they're right—maybe you *should* be doing more. Maybe you *aren't* trying hard enough. Maybe you *are* a disappointment.

But hold on. Let's take a step back.

What if—and hear me out—you were never the problem? What if the real issue is that the world got way too comfortable expecting miracles from you? What if all this pressure isn't proof that you're failing, but proof that you've set the bar so ridiculously high that people forget you're human?

So, congratulations! You're a disappointment—at least, by the world's impossible standards. But maybe—just maybe—it's time to stop chasing an applause that was never meant to last forever.

The Grand Welcome to Teenage Expectations

At first, it feels like a challenge. You tell yourself, "I'll just work a little harder." You pull all-nighters, turn into a human calculator, and hope that a 95% will finally earn you that magical thing called "appreciation." But guess what? "Beta, where are the remaining 5 marks?"

It's like running a marathon where the finish line keeps moving, except instead of a medal, you get another lecture. You could be saving the world, but if you forget to make your bed, you're still a disappointment. And if you think you can avoid the comparison trap, think again. You could single-handedly save the planet from climate change, and the first reaction from your family would still be: *"Yes, but can you also become a doctor?"*

And so, the chase begins. Not just for **marks**—oh no, that would be too simple. The chase for validation. For that slight **nod of approval** from your parents, that rare and mythical creature known as "Good job, beta." The problem? It's like trying to catch a train that keeps speeding up. The moment you think you've caught up, the expectations shift.

First, it's about **good grades.** Then, it's about **being "all-rounder."** Excelling in sports, music, dance, debate, origami, astrophysics, cooking, and probably inventing time travel while you're at it. Because apparently, being "just smart" is not enough. You have to be **smart but also talented, charming,**

obedient, physically fit, socially active, and preferably already on track to become a CEO.

Oh, and **don't forget to sleep well, drink water, and have a social life too.** (Hilarious, right?)

The "Log Kya Kahenge" Olympics

Of course, **the real judges of your worth are not even your parents**—they're the **entire extended family plus random aunties who have a PhD in Judgmental Studies.** These are people who appear out of nowhere, like unpaid background actors in your life movie, only to ask intrusive questions like:

> "Beta, what are your plans after 12th?" (Surviving, Aunty. My plan is **to survive.**)
> "How much percentage did Sharma ji's son get?" (Why do I look like Sharma ji's exam invigilator??)
> "Engineering or medical?" (How about **peace and quiet** instead?)

And heaven forbid you choose something unconventional—like writing, filmmaking, music, psychology, or **basically anything that doesn't involve a stethoscope or an engineering degree.** Because then, you're officially **a rebel.** A disappointment. The reason Aunt Sunita will shake her head in dramatic sorrow at the next family function.

And you start wondering—**what exactly is the goal here?** At what point do you finally "win" in this game of expectations? Because every time you hit a milestone, **the bar moves again.**

The Art of Being "Not Enough"

Got a 95%? **Where are the remaining 5 marks?**
Got into a top college? **But why not the best one?**
Got a great job? **But when are you getting married?**
Got married? **But when are the kids coming?**
Had kids? **But when are they getting married?**

It **never ends.** There's always something more to prove, always another level to unlock in this **never-ending, stress-**

filled, judgmental video game called "Life According to Society."

And the worst part? **We start believing it.** We internalize the idea that no matter what we do, it's never quite enough. That our worth is tied to achievements, as if we're walking report cards instead of human beings. That **our happiness is secondary to society's expectations.**

But what if we stopped playing along?

Rewriting the Rules

What if we stopped chasing the approval of people who will never be satisfied? What if, instead of running a race that leads nowhere, we just…**quit the race?**

What if we decided that **our happiness, our passion, and our peace matter more than society's approval?** That success isn't just about high-paying jobs and gold medals—it's also about **waking up without anxiety, doing what we love, and having the audacity to live on our own terms?**

What if we dared to **be enough, just as we are?**

Because, in the end, the real question isn't, **"What do others expect of me?"**

The real question is, **"What do I expect from myself?"**

And **that**—just that—changes everything.

The 'Sharma Ji's Kid' Paradox

There's always a Sharma ji's kid. You know the one. The mythical creature who always scores 99%, plays three instruments, and probably discovered a new planet over the summer.

Even if you do something incredible—win a competition, get a scholarship, invent a teleportation device—someone will find a way to say, "Haan, but Sharma ji's beta did it first." If Sharma ji's kid ever trips, falls, or fails at something, we wouldn't know. They're basically a legend at this point—half-student, half-myth, 100% your biggest existential crisis.

Here's the thing—**has anyone actually seen Sharma ji's kid?** Like, in real life? Not just as a name floating around in conversations, but as a **breathing, walking human being?**

No? Thought so.

For all we know, they might just be a **social construct created to keep us humble.** Some say they exist, some say they don't, and the rest of us are just caught in this **never-ending chase for perfection.**

And even if they're real, **why are we competing with them?** Life isn't some leaderboard where we need to beat an imaginary opponent to win. **Your life = your journey.** Just because Sharma ji's kid is playing their game at **insane difficulty mode** doesn't mean you have to. Here's a wild thought: **What if we don't even WANT their life?**

Sure, their achievements look amazing on paper, but let's break it down:

Do they have time to **binge-watch Netflix at 2 AM**?

Can they **laugh at dumb memes for hours**?

Have they **argued about whether pineapple belongs on pizza?**

Do they have the **freedom to make silly mistakes and just** ***live*****? Doubt it.**

There's something really powerful about **choosing your own path, even if it isn't the "perfect" one.** Maybe you're not aiming for a 99% in every exam, but you have a passion that makes you happy. Maybe you aren't playing three instruments, but you're writing, designing, building, or creating something that makes your soul light up.

Maybe, just maybe, **you're doing just fine.**

Rewriting the Rules

At the end of the day, what matters isn't **being better than Sharma ji's kid—it's being better than the 'you' from yesterday.**

(Deep, right? Bet Sharma ji's kid didn't think of that.)

The next time someone brings them up in conversation, just smile and say:
"That's great for them! But I'm writing my own story."

And honestly? **That's the biggest flex of all.**

The Marks vs. Talent Battle

Here's a fun fact: The world wants you to "follow your passion." But only if your passion comes with a stable salary, a prestigious title, and a LinkedIn-worthy success story.

Got a talent for music? "Nice hobby, beta, but what about IIT?" Want to be a writer? "Good, but also prepare for UPSC." Love photography? "Great! Now become an engineer and do photography on weekends."

Society loves talent. It just doesn't love the risk that comes with it. It's like asking a fish to swim but only if it's also willing to climb a tree, juggle fire, and solve a calculus problem while doing it. No pressure, though.

The Burnout No One Talks About

Between school, coaching, competitions, and the endless pressure of being "the best," burnout is inevitable. But no one talks about it. Because admitting you're exhausted is the same as admitting defeat.

So, you keep going. You force yourself to function on caffeine and willpower. You suppress the panic attacks, the self-doubt, the fear of failing. You tell yourself, "Just a little more. Then I'll be happy."

Spoiler alert: That "little more" never ends. It's like trying to fill a bucket with a hole at the bottom. No matter how much you pour in, it always leaks out. And guess who's left carrying that empty bucket, wondering why they feel drained all the time? That's right—YOU.

You know how people say, **"Follow your passion!"**? Yeah, well, they actually mean **"Follow your passion… but only if it fits our definition of success."**

I took **Non-Med** because, like every ambitious student, I thought it would open doors to endless possibilities. And, let's be honest, back then, **"possibilities" basically meant engineering or medicine.**

But then, I had a wild, rebellious thought: **"What if I become a lawyer?"**

That's when the real drama started.

Law? A **girl** studying **law**? Suddenly, everyone turned into self-appointed career advisors with PhDs in **"What will people say?"** studies.

"Girls who are lawyers never get married!" Ah yes, because marriage proposals are strictly reserved for engineers and doctors. **"Lawyers speak too much."** And? You want me to argue for free? **"It's not a good job for a girl."** Sorry, I didn't realize passion had a gender.

I tried. I really did. But after a few rounds of unsolicited advice, **even I started doubting myself.** Maybe law wasn't a good idea? Maybe I should just **sit for engineering exams** like a good Non-Med student?

Spoiler alert: Big mistake.

I **barely made it through that phase.** Not because I wasn't capable, but because my **mental health took a nosedive.** The constant pressure, the expectations, the feeling that I was running a race I didn't even want to be in—it drained me.

So I took a step back. I thought, **"Okay, maybe engineering isn't my thing, maybe law isn't 'acceptable' (according to society), so what now?"**

That's when the idea hit me—**moving abroad for teaching.**

A **stable career? Absolutely.**
Financial independence? Even better.
A chance to escape the judgmental aunties? A dream come true.

But the thing is, **I'm still not giving up on law.** Even after choosing to **pursue teaching first, I know I'll come**

back to my passion. Because, at the end of the day, **no one should have to sacrifice their dreams just to make other people comfortable.**

So yeah, I'm still figuring it out. Still pushing through. **Still chasing what makes me happy.**

And if that means breaking a few stereotypes along the way? **Even better.**

The Realization (And the Messy Middle Ground)

At some point, something shifts. Maybe you break down one day. Maybe you have an epiphany at 3 AM while overanalyzing your life choices. Or maybe you just get tired of living like a machine.

You realize you'll never truly satisfy everyone. No matter how hard you try, someone will always think you could have done better. And maybe that's okay.

Maybe success isn't about perfect marks, glowing report cards, or being the best in a crowd of tired overachievers. Maybe success is about doing what actually makes you feel alive.

Maybe success is realizing that the people who truly care about you won't measure your worth in decimals and percentages. Maybe success is choosing peace over perfection.

And maybe—just maybe—that's enough.

Or at the very least, it's a great excuse to dramatically flop onto your bed, listen to sad music like you're in a coming-of-age movie, and stare at the ceiling like it holds the secrets of the universe. Bonus points if you also eat ice cream straight from the tub while questioning the meaning of life.

Perfect? No. Relatable? Absolutely. Now pass the spoon.

The Grand Plot Twist (A.K.A. The Teen Life Survival Guide)

So, after all the existential dread, the academic chaos, the "Sharma Ji's kid" comparisons, the talent vs. marks battle, the burnout, and the identity crisis disguised as career planning—

what's the final answer? What's the grand, life-changing lesson?

Well, let's get one thing straight: *There is none.*

If you were waiting for a magical moment where everything makes sense and all your problems dissolve into thin air—sorry to disappoint, but life isn't a Disney movie. No wise old mentor is about to hand you a prophecy that explains your entire purpose. No dramatic background music will start playing when you make a life-changing decision (unless you personally add it to your playlist, which is highly recommended).

But here's what *does* happen: **You realize that none of this was ever about being "the best."**

At some point, you get tired of chasing perfection like it's a limited-edition sneaker drop. You get tired of stressing over what relatives, society, or random neighbors who can't mind their own business think. You get tired of acting like your whole existence depends on a percentage written on a piece of paper.

And that's when the real plot twist happens: **You start living for yourself.**

You stop trying to win some imaginary competition that no one even knows the rules to. You stop feeling guilty for wanting things outside of the traditional "successful" path. You realize that no matter how much you try to be perfect, someone *will* always find a reason to say, *"Hmm… but have you considered being EVEN better?"* And honestly? That's exhausting.

So, what do you do instead?

You start making choices that actually make you happy—even if they confuse some people. Even if they make your parents do that deep sigh of disappointment. Even if it means switching paths, taking risks, or—dare I say—**not having your entire life mapped out at 17.**

Because guess what? **No one really has it figured out.** Some are just better at faking it.

And if you still feel lost? That's okay. If you don't have a solid five-year plan? That's okay too. If you fail, change your mind, try something new, and then change your mind *again*—congratulations, you're human.

So, go ahead. Follow your passion. Or don't. Take risks. Or play it safe. Move abroad for teaching but still plan to do law later because passion doesn't expire. Sit for an engineering exam just to realize it's *definitely* not for you. Confuse the hell out of everyone by changing your career goals like outfit choices. **It's your life.**

And at the end of the day, when you look back, make sure that *you* were the one writing the story—not society, not random judgmental aunties, not some invisible scoreboard of success.

Because the real secret? **Nobody actually cares as much as you think they do.** So stop overthinking it. Live a little. Maybe even a lot. And definitely keep some ice cream in the freezer for all future existential crises—you're gonna need it.

CHAPTER-3

Chapter 3: The Struggle for Identity

Ah, teenage years—the golden era of self-discovery, deep thoughts at 2 AM, and asking yourself, "Who am I?" while aggressively scrolling through memes. One minute, you feel like the main character, walking in slow motion to your favorite song. The next? You're lying in bed, overanalysing a conversation from three weeks ago, convinced you embarrassed yourself so badly you might need to change your identity and move to another country.

No one warns you about the identity glitches that happen mid-conversation. Like when you're in a debate, passionately defending your stance, and halfway through, you realize—wait. Do I even believe this? Or did I just commit to this personality for the sake of the argument? Too late now. Guess I'm a philosopher.

And then, there's the *unexpected identity-shattering moments.* You could be minding your business, happily existing, when suddenly, a random comment from someone— "You're always so quiet" or "Wow, you've changed"—sends you into an existential spiral. Am I quiet? Did I change? Who was I before? Who am I now? Should I go on a soul-searching trip? (Translation: watch five hours of coming-of-age movies and pretend to relate).

And don't even get me started on the *phases.* Every teen has gone through at least three of these:

The "Deep and Mysterious" Phase – You read poetry, stare out of windows dramatically, and post cryptic song lyrics on your stories. People ask if you're okay. You say, "I just see the world differently now."

The "Rebel Without a Cause" Phase – You decide you're a rule-breaker. You do something wild… like *not use a bookmark while reading.* Chaos.

The "Hyper-Optimistic Self-Improvement" Phase – You wake up one day and decide this is *your era.* You'll eat healthy, work out, journal, and become a morning person. It lasts three days.

The "Maybe I'm a Completely Different Person" Phase – You get a haircut. Boom. New personality. New life. (Same you, though).

At the end of the day, identity isn't something you *find* like a missing sock under your bed. You don't just wake up one morning and go, "Ah yes, I am now a fully developed individual with a stable personality." No. You will continue to change, evolve, and sometimes, yes, embarrass yourself *very publicly* in the process.

And that's okay. Because maybe, just *maybe*, the real "you" isn't some final, polished version of yourself waiting at the finish line. Maybe it's all the awkward phases, the dramatic moments, the random bursts of inspiration, and the times you had to reinvent yourself after a particularly bad outfit choice.

So, who are you? The answer, my friend, is always changing. And honestly? That's the best part.

Friendships: Lifelines or Landmines?

Friendships in your teenage years are intense. They feel like soul connections, ride-or-die pacts, the kind of thing you'd see in movies. You share secrets, inside jokes, and existential crises. But then—plot twist—things get complicated. Maybe you feel like you're always the one making the effort. Maybe they make a joke at your expense, and it stings more than it should. Maybe they start hanging out with someone else, and suddenly, you're the afterthought.

No one prepares you for how friendships can sometimes feel like a full-time job—except there's no salary, just emotional roller coasters and occasional passive-aggressive Instagram captions.

And don't even get me started on the *group chats.* One minute, they're buzzing with memes and chaotic energy. The next, you realize you've missed 472 messages, and when you finally catch up, the conversation has already moved on.

You know what's funny? How you can be *so sure* that you and someone are going to be good friends forever. Like, you truly believe it. *This is my person.* We'll grow old together, call each other in the middle of the night to complain about life, and have inside jokes that make literally no sense to anyone else. You go through phases together—the "we are the main characters" phase, the "we are so different but that's what makes it work" phase, and the "no one understands me like she does" phase. You start believing this person is your ride-or-die, your soul sister, your *forever.*

Until… it turns out they're just a temporary character in your story.

At first, I brushed it off. It's easy to do that when you care about someone. Maybe I misheard. Maybe I'm just sensitive. Maybe she didn't *really* mean it that way. She teases me too much? That's just her personality. She makes me feel stupid when I talk about things I love? Oh well, maybe I'm just *overreacting.* She always makes herself seem superior, like my feelings are inconvenient, like anything I say that doesn't fit her version of things is *wrong*? Okay… maybe that's just how friendships are.

Right?

And I almost convinced myself. Almost.

Until one day, she crossed a line. Not with a joke, not with a casual tease, but with a single, thoughtless, sharp comment about someone who is my close one. Not me. Not my grades, not my choices, not the way I talk or act or look. She aimed at someone close to me. Someone who means more to me than she ever could.

That's when it hit me—she wasn't joking. She was never *just joking.*

See, I let things slide when it was about me. I made excuses. *She doesn't mean it like that. Maybe I'm being too sensitive. Maybe I should just let it go.* But the moment she dragged someone I care about into it? Oh, *that* was when the silence ended. That's when I finally stood up and said, "Hey. That's not okay."

She said, *"Oh my god, why are you making a fight out of nothing? I was just joking."*

Right. Joking. The magical, all-powerful word that's supposed to erase accountability. The "get out of jail free" card of people who say whatever they want and expect you to just *deal with it.*

But here's the thing. *Loyalty is not a joke to me, ma'am.*

You don't get to talk bad about the people I care about and expect me to sit there, nodding like an idiot. You don't get to insult me over and over and then act *shocked* when I finally push back. You don't get to throw stones and then pretend you didn't mean to break the glass.

Because here's what I've learned—if someone only values you when you let them walk all over you, that's not a friendship. That's an audience. And I? I refuse to be part of their entertainment lineup.

I used to be the person who let things go, just so I wouldn't "cause drama." But guess what? Sometimes, taking a stand means being called dramatic. Sometimes, being *loyal* means losing people. And sometimes, the kindest thing you can do for yourself is to walk away, not with anger, not with resentment, but with *peace.*

So yeah, I've changed. But honestly? I like this version of me better. Friendship is such a weird concept if you really think about it. Like, one day, you're just vibing, living your life, and then—bam!—someone new sits next to you in class, asks to borrow a pen, and suddenly, they're your ride-or-die for the next few years. It's like an arranged marriage, but with inside jokes and matching phone wallpapers.

And at first, it's all sunshine and rainbows. You share notes, gossip about the people you don't like (but will still smile at), and take cringe selfies you promise to delete but never do. You hype each other up in the comments of Instagram posts like it's a full-time job—*"Omg queen, slay, you own this planet"*. You're basically inseparable.

Until one day, *poof*, they're gone. Maybe they found a new group. Maybe they started acting weird. Maybe you had an argument over something small, and suddenly, the friendship that felt like a forever thing is now a "what happened?"

Friendship breakups are so underrated in the heartbreak department. If someone breaks your heart in a relationship, the world understands—you cry, you watch sad movies, people check in on you. But if you lose a friend? You're expected to just *move on*. No one tells you that you'll randomly hear a song that reminds you of them and feel a tiny ache in your chest. No one warns you about the sudden urge to text them when something funny happens, only to remember that you don't *talk anymore*.

But here's the real kicker: you never see it coming. One day, you're hyping her up to talk to her crush, the next, she's lowkey making fun of you to impress them. One moment, you think she's laughing *with* you, the next, you realize… oh. No. She's laughing *at* you.

And we sit there, letting it happen, because God forbid we be called "too sensitive." I mean, apparently, having basic self-respect is *so dramatic*.

But let me tell you something about me: **I take loyalty seriously.** I don't find it cute or quirky when a friend makes fun of me in front of others just for a cheap laugh. I don't think it's *just a joke* when someone crosses a line and then gaslights me into thinking I'm the one overreacting. That's not friendship. That's a stand-up comedy show at *my expense*, and sorry, but I never bought a ticket for that.

And yet, it's funny how friendships work. Sometimes, they're a slow fade, like an old text thread you never really closed, but one day, you just… stop replying. Other times, it's like a grand explosion—you say one wrong thing, and suddenly, you're the villain in a drama you didn't even audition for.

And let's be real, friendships are *weird*. You'll be best friends for five years and then break up because they borrowed your hoodie and "forgot" to return it for six months (which, let's be honest, means they had no intention of returning it at all). Or you'll meet someone in the school washroom, bond over your mutual hatred for PE class, and boom—you have a new soulmate.

And then, there are those friendships that just… wither. No big fight, no drama—just life. You used to know everything about each other, now it's just, *Hey, what's up?* on birthdays, followed by a three-day delay in response. And that's okay. Some people are meant to be in your story for a few chapters, not the whole book. And as much as it stings to see the pages turn, you can't force them to stay when the plot has already moved on.

Because at the end of the day, friendship isn't about who you started with. It's about who sticks around. It's about who actually *listens* to your rants instead of waiting for their turn to speak. Who hypes you up *even when no one's watching*. Who doesn't call you sensitive when you tell them something hurt you.

Real friends don't make you feel like a side character in your own life. They don't insult you for fun, test your patience just to see when you'll snap, or act like *your feelings are a problem* instead of taking accountability for how they made you feel.

So here's to the friendships that *don't* make you feel like you're constantly auditioning for a place in their lives. Here's to the ones where you can send the most unhinged texts at 3 AM and know they'll just respond with *same*. The ones who look at you and go, *That's my person. That's my weirdo.*

And to the ones who never deserved your loyalty? Let them go. You don't need to cross oceans for someone who wouldn't even step in a puddle for you.

Because friendship should feel safe. It should feel like home. Not like a never-ending test you keep failing.

And if that makes me *too sensitive*? Then fine. I'll take that over being a doormat. Any. Day.

The Validation Game: Likes, Attention, and The Great Identity Crisis

Admit it. You've posted a story, checked who viewed it, and then acted like you didn't care. Or maybe you posted something, got fewer likes than expected, and suddenly felt like deleting your entire existence. Welcome to the modern age of self-worth being tied to numbers!

But here's the thing: No matter how many likes you get, there will always be that little voice whispering, "Could've been more." And even when people hype you up, you'll still find a way to convince yourself it's not enough. Why? Because somewhere along the way, we started mistaking validation for self-worth. Spoiler alert: They're not the same thing. **The Pressure to "Fit In" (Whatever That Means)**

If you've ever stood in front of a mirror and thought, "If I was just a little taller, a little skinnier, had better skin, or maybe a completely different face, then I'd be happier," congratulations! You've experienced *The Universal Teenage Insecurity Crisis*™.

Oof, the things we tell ourselves, right? For the longest time, I genuinely believed that because I was underweight, people assumed I wasn't *a good person.* Like, forget personality, kindness, or whether I help old people cross the street—nope. Apparently, if you don't have enough meat on your bones, society collectively decides you lack *character development.*

And I let that thought sit in my brain rent-free for *years.* Until one day, mid-overthinking session, it hit me: **since when did weight become a moral compass?** Like, oh no, she's a few kilos lighter, she must be evil. What's next? Judging people's kindness based on their shoe size?

And that's when I realized something even bigger: we all have that *one thing* we convince ourselves makes us *less*—less lovable, less worthy, less *good.* Some people think they're too quiet to be interesting, too loud to be taken seriously, too awkward to be loved properly. But tell me, does any of that determine if you pray silently when an ambulance passes? Does it decide if your heart aches when you see a little kid barefoot on a freezing sidewalk? Does it stop you from paying for someone's meal just because *they never got the chance to experience that kind of kindness before*?

Because I do all of that. And that means I *am* love. Not the Instagram-quote, aesthetic-post, "self-love journey " kind of love. I mean real, messy, unfiltered *love*. The kind that doesn't need an audience or a "like" count to exist.

And guess what? **So are you.** Not because of how you look, or how people perceive you, or how well you perform in the *Validation Olympics*. But because of how you *care*. How you *feel*. How you *show up* for people, even when no one's watching.

And if the world ever tries to make you feel *less* because of some random, meaningless standard? Remind them: *I don't need to be "enough" for you, because I am already more than enough for the people who matter.*

And most importantly, for *me*.

We've all been there. Comparing ourselves to the "perfect" people on social media, wondering why we don't look effortlessly flawless, forgetting that those perfect people also spent 40 minutes choosing the right angle and used three different filters.

And confidence? That thing we all pretend to have? Turns out, it's not about being flawless. It's about faking it so well that even you start believing it. (And if that fails, there's always the classic trick: walking with AirPods in, pretending you're in a music video.)

The Pressure to "Fit In" (Whatever That Means)

If you've ever stood in front of a mirror and thought, "If I was just a little taller, a little skinnier, had better skin, or maybe a completely different face, then I'd be happier," congratulations! You've experienced *The Universal Teenage Insecurity Crisis*™.

Oof, the things we tell ourselves, right? For the longest time, I genuinely believed that because I was underweight, people assumed I wasn't *a good person*. Like, forget personality, kindness, or whether I help old people cross the street—nope. Apparently, if you don't have enough meat on your bones, society collectively decides you lack *character development*.

And I let that thought sit in my brain rent-free for *years*. Until one day, mid-overthinking session, it hit me: **since when did weight become a moral compass?** Like, oh no, she's a few kilos lighter, she must be evil. What's next? Judging people's kindness based on their shoe size?

And that's when I realized something even bigger: we all have that *one thing* we convince ourselves makes us *less*—less lovable, less worthy, less *good*. Some people think they're too quiet to be interesting, too loud to be taken seriously, too awkward to be loved properly. But tell me, does any of that determine if you pray silently when an ambulance passes? Does it decide if your heart aches when you see a little kid barefoot on a freezing sidewalk? Does it stop you from paying for someone's meal just because *they never got the chance to experience that kind of kindness before*?

Because I do all of that. And that means I *am* love. Not the Instagram-quote, aesthetic-post, "self-love journey " kind of love. I mean real, messy, unfiltered *love*. The kind that doesn't need an audience or a "like" count to exist.

And guess what? **So are you.** Not because of how you look, or how people perceive you, or how well you perform in the *Validation Olympics*. But because of how you *care*. How you *feel*. How you *show up* for people, even when no one's watching.

And if the world ever tries to make you feel *less* because of some random, meaningless standard? Remind them: *I don't need to be "enough" for you, because I am already more than enough for the people who matter.*

And most importantly, for *me*.

We've all been there. Comparing ourselves to the "perfect" people on social media, wondering why we don't look effortlessly flawless, forgetting that those perfect people also spent 40 minutes choosing the right angle and used three different filters.

And confidence? That thing we all pretend to have? Turns out, it's not about being flawless. It's about faking it so well that even you start believing it. (And if that fails, there's always the classic trick: walking with AirPods in, pretending you're in a music video.)

Now, let's talk about one of the weirdest human experiences—trying to infiltrate an already-established friend group. It's like walking into a party where everyone already knows the inside jokes, and you're just standing there, laughing along, hoping no one realizes you have no idea what's going on.

The first few days? You're basically a background character. Nodding, laughing at jokes you don't understand, and praying they don't notice you've been silently sipping your drink for 10 minutes just to avoid looking awkward. Then, when you *finally* think you're fitting in, boom—someone hits you with, **"Remember that time we—"** and suddenly, you're an alien in a foreign land.

Now, this part? This one *really* gets me.

I've had so many female friends pull the classic:

"Wait, are you saying I can't curse because I'm a girl??" As if that was ever the argument. No, ma'am, my issue isn't with *who* is cursing—it's with *why* everyone suddenly thinks it's a personality trait.

And you know what's even wilder? I once knew a girl who spoke *every* curse word you could think of—especially the ones that involve people's *mothers and sisters*. The *worst* kind. The ones that, if said in front of an actual mother or sister, could get you disowned from society.

And this girl? She was once a **topper.** (Maybe still is. I wouldn't know—I had to distance myself before my brain started leaking out of my ears.)

But the thing is, hearing *those* words come from *anyone*, let alone someone who used to be known for their intellect, was… unsettling. Like, how do you go from being a person who once debated over philosophical theories to casually tossing around words that could start a full-fledged family feud?

And listen, I get it—people change. We grow, we evolve, we pick up new habits. But this wasn't growth. This was *regression disguised as rebellion.*

Because let's be honest: If the only thing your personality has going for it is a dictionary of expletives, **what even is your personality?** Like, are you *actually* funny, or do you just throw in a curse word and hope people mistake it for humor? Are you *actually* confident, or do you just swear aggressively to cover up the fact that you don't know what else to say?

It's like some people think cursing excessively makes them "bold" or "badass." But what's bold about lacking vocabulary? What's badass about using the same 4 words over and over until they lose all meaning?

And let's not ignore the hypocrisy: The *same* people who say "I can curse too; I'm not a delicate little girl" are often the first ones to get offended over the smallest thing. Like, oh, you can verbally obliterate someone's entire family lineage, but the moment someone makes a *mild* joke about you, suddenly it's **"That was uncalled for."**

So no, it's not about whether you're a girl, a guy, or a talking parrot. It's about the fact that some people have mistaken *shock value* for *having an actual presence.*

And in a world where everyone thinks they have to be the loudest to be heard, sometimes the real power is in *choosing what not to say.*

At the end of the day, you don't need to listen to anyone or try to do things just to "look cool." Think before you speak, because no matter how many books you read, the way you carry yourself will always decide whether you look **educated or just educated-on-paper.**

The Things We Don't Talk About (But Should)

Mental health struggles in your teenage years are like that one messy drawer in your room—you know it's there, but you'd rather not deal with it.

The pressure to be okay all the time? Exhausting. The fear of admitting you're *not* okay? Even worse. Sometimes, the hardest thing isn't dealing with your emotions—it's figuring out *how* to talk about them without feeling like a burden.

So instead, you say "I'm fine" when you're not. You laugh at jokes that hit a little too close to home. You make memes out of your own struggles because, hey, if you turn it into a joke, it's not that serious, right?

But here's the thing: It *is* serious. And it's okay to admit that. You're not "too sensitive." You're not "just overthinking." You're a human being figuring life out in a world that makes it ridiculously hard to do so.

So, Who Are You, Really?

Here's the plot twist no one tells you: No one really *knows* who they are at 16. Or 18. Or 25. Or even 40.

You don't have to have all the answers right now. You don't need to fit into a box. You don't need to be the smartest, funniest, prettiest, or most talented. You just need to be *you*—messy, complicated, figuring-it-out, still-learning *you.*

Because, spoiler alert: That's more than enough.

CHAPTER-4

Chapter: The Things We Don't Talk About (But Should)

Teenage years are like trying to charge your phone with a half-broken charger—you're not entirely sure what's working, what's not, and why everything feels like it's about to catch fire at any given moment. You're supposed to be *living your best life*, but somehow, instead of the movie montage where you're thriving, it feels more like a chaotic blooper reel where you're just trying to make it through the day without embarrassing yourself too badly.

One minute, you're laughing so hard you can't breathe. The next, you're lying in bed at 3 AM, staring at the ceiling like, *Did I actually say that in 2019? Should I legally change my name and flee the country?* And somehow, both of these things feel equally important. And then there's the constant pressure to have everything figured out—like, sorry, am I supposed to know my life plan when I still have to sing the alphabet in my head to remember if L comes before M? Adults keep asking, *"What do you want to do in the future?"* as if I even know what I'm doing this weekend. (*Hint: probably overthinking something dumb while aggressively snacking.*)

Let's not even get started on social interactions. One moment, you're vibing with your friends, feeling like the main character. The next, you say something slightly weird, and your brain is like, *That's it. We're never speaking again. Ever.* And suddenly, you're questioning your entire personality.

Oh, and the overanalyzing? A full-time job. That one "K." text from your friend? Might as well start drafting an apology letter for whatever imaginary crime you think you committed. Someone doesn't reply for five hours? Obviously, they hate you. (*Or, you know, they're just busy being a normal human.*) But no, your brain insists it's the beginning of your social downfall.

And confidence? Ha. Some days, you feel like you could run the world. Other days, making eye contact with the waiter feels like an extreme sport. And yet, somehow, you're expected to strut through life like you have it all under control.

The truth? None of us do. We're all just winging it, hoping no one notices. And honestly, that's kind of comforting.

The Silent Chaos of Growing Up

Mental health struggles in our teenage years are like that one junk drawer in your house—overstuffed, chaotic, and full of things you don't know how to deal with. And instead of organizing it, you just shove more stuff in there and pretend it's fine. (*Spoiler alert: it is, in fact, NOT fine.*)

The pressure to be okay all the time? Exhausting. The fear of admitting you're *not* okay? Somehow even worse. And since society decided that showing emotions = weakness, most of us have mastered the art of looking totally chill while internally having an existential crisis.

So, instead of saying, *"I feel like my brain is drowning,"* you just drop a casual *"I'm fine"* in a voice so fake even Siri would be like, *Girl, no you're not.*

So, instead of saying, *"I feel like my brain is drowning,"* you just drop a casual *"I'm fine"* in a voice so fake even Siri would be like, *Girl, no you're not.* And then you move on, pretending that overthinking your entire existence at 2 AM is totally normal behavior.

Speaking of 2 AM—why is it that the second my head hits the pillow, my brain decides it's the perfect time to run a full-fledged documentary titled *"Every Embarrassing Thing You've Ever Done: Director's Cut"*? Like, oh, you wanted sleep? Too bad, let's relive that awkward conversation from five years ago in *high definition.* And just when I think I can finally doze off, my brain is like, *"Wait, but what if you fail in life, end up broke, and have to live in a cardboard box?"* Love that for me.

Anxiety is basically having a personal alarm system that goes off at the most unnecessary times. *Dropped a spoon? Omg, everyone definitely saw and now they think you're weird. Texted someone and they didn't reply in 0.2 seconds? They obviously hate you. Made a tiny mistake? Great, now you're a disgrace to your entire bloodline.* I wish I were kidding, but this is *literally* my daily thought process.

Some days, I wake up and feel like I need therapy, a long vacation, and a whole new personality all at once. I get irrationally annoyed at the *smallest* things—like when my charger stops working unless I twist it at a perfect 37-degree angle, or when someone takes too long to type a reply. What are you writing? A novel? Just say "okay" and move on. And don't even get me started on the people who tell me, *"Just be positive!"* Oh, really? Why didn't I think of that? Let me just switch off my anxiety like a bedside lamp. Genius.

One of the biggest scams of growing up is that you're expected to have it all figured out when, in reality, most of us are just out here making it up as we go. People say, *"Enjoy your teenage years, they're the best time of your life!"* which is hilarious because I've never been more confused, stressed, and mentally exhausted in my entire existence. It's like being thrown into a game with no instructions, and just when you start getting the hang of it, life updates the software, and now the rules don't make sense anymore.

And then there's the whole identity crisis thing. Some days, I wake up and feel like I know exactly who I am. Other days, I stare at my reflection like I'm a side character in my own life, wondering if I'm actually interesting or if I just have cool earrings. Social media makes it worse. One minute, I'm totally fine with myself, and the next, I'm spiraling because some random stranger on Instagram has perfect skin, a perfect life, and somehow looks flawless even in candids. Meanwhile, I can't even blink without looking like I'm mid-sneeze.

Look, I know you don't *need* advice. You probably didn't even *ask* for it. But I have to say this because I went through it, and if someone had told me this earlier, maybe I wouldn't have spent so many nights staring at my ceiling, questioning my entire existence.

So here it is: **You are not running out of time.**

I know it *feels* like you have to figure out your whole life right now, like every decision you make is some irreversible contract. But it's not. You can change. You can grow. You can mess up and start over. Life isn't a test where you only get one chance to fill in the right bubble. It's more like those *choose your own adventure* books—if one path doesn't work out, you can always flip back a few pages and try again.

And another thing—**stop treating yourself like your own worst enemy.** You wouldn't talk to your best friend the way you talk to yourself, so why do you let your brain bully you? You're doing *way better* than you think.

And finally—this one's important—**don't let the world convince you that being kind makes you weak, or that being emotional makes you dramatic.** Having feelings isn't a flaw. It's what makes you *human.* And in a world that tries so hard to make you numb, *feeling things* is a rebellion in itself.

That's it. That's the advice. You can ignore it, pretend you never read it, or come back to it in five years when it finally makes sense. Either way, just know—you're gonna be okay. Even if you don't believe it yet.

We Make Jokes About Our Trauma Because… What Else Are We Supposed to Do?

Let's be real—at this point, half of us communicate exclusively in self-deprecating humor and existential crisis memes. You could be going through an absolute mental breakdown, but instead of talking about it, you just send a meme that says, *"haha I'm so mentally stable"* and hope no one asks follow-up questions. And if they do? Just hit them with a *"lol dw, I'm fine"* and immediately change the subject. (It's practically a reflex at this point.)

Because actually talking about feelings? That's uncharted territory, my friend. We joke, we deflect, we send *skull emojis* to express how dead inside we feel—but the second someone says, *"Hey, are you actually okay?"* our brains go into full system shutdown.

Somewhere along the way, we collectively decided that turning our pain into a joke is easier than admitting it exists. So instead of saying, *"I feel like my brain is drowning in stress and self-doubt,"* we just drop a casual *"lol I might just run away and become a tree"* and move on. And it works... kind of. Until it's 3 AM, and suddenly, the same brain that was cracking jokes all day is like, *Hey, remember that embarrassing thing you did in 2015? Let's relive that in HD with full surround sound.*

And that's the thing. We joke. We deflect. We pretend. But deep down, we all know—there's only so much pretending we can do before it catches up to us.

For the longest time, I was a professional pretender. Joking around with Dad like I had zero worries, annoying Mumma just for fun, acting like my biggest problem in life was whether my charger was working or not. But deep down? I was one overthinking session away from completely short-circuiting. I'd crack a joke about failing at life, say "haha I'm so done" at least five times a day, and somehow convince myself that if I laughed about my stress, it didn't *actually* exist. (Spoiler: it did. It really, really did.) But admitting that? Pfft. Too risky. Instead, I'd distract myself with memes, binge-watch random YouTube videos at 2 AM, and tell myself *tomorrow* I'd deal with it. Spoiler again: I didn't.

The thing is, I've always been sensitive. And I still am. And honestly? Good. Somewhere along the way, the world decided that feeling things deeply = weakness. Like, oh no, you have *emotions*? Tragic. But you know what's actually tragic? Pretending you don't. It's *not* wrong to cry when things get heavy. It's *not* embarrassing to have actual feelings. It's literally part of being human. And I'd rather be the person who cares too much than the one who doesn't care at all. So yeah, I'll probably still overthink things, still stress about my future, still cry over movies I *wasn't even watching properly*. But you know what? At least I'm real.

Somewhere along the way, people took "equality" and played a game of broken telephone with it. Like, yes, feminism is about equal rights, equal opportunities—but *equal* means *equal*, not flipping the script and creating a whole new problem. We say we want fairness, yet we tell boys, *"Be a man, don't cry,"* like emotions are some top-secret, women-only VIP club. Sorry, but last I checked, men also have a nervous system. They also feel things. And yet, society has this weird obsession with making them act like emotionally unavailable robots. Like, bro, if you stub your toe, you're allowed to scream in pain. You're not gonna lose your "man card" because a tear slipped out.

And let's talk about this whole *"men should be strong"* thing. *Strong how?* Physically? Emotionally? Strong enough to carry all their trauma in silence because the world told them that's what "real men" do? If a guy opens up about his feelings, he's "weak." But if he doesn't, he's "cold and distant." Y'all, which one is it? Because right now, it just sounds like an elaborate setup to make sure men are stuck in an endless loop of *"be tough but not too tough but also don't be soft but also express yourself but actually no, don't"*. Like, pick a struggle.

Oh, it starts *early*. Like, before boys even learn how to tie their shoes, they learn that crying is some sort of felony. Little Timmy falls off his bike? *"Get up, don't cry! Be a man!"* Meanwhile, Little Tina stubs her toe, and suddenly there's a full emotional support squad rushing in like *"Oh no, sweetheart, does it hurt? Want ice cream?"* And just like that, BOOM—society hands boys an invisible handbook titled **"How to Emotionally Suppress Yourself Like a Proper Man™."**

Then, fast forward to adulthood, and suddenly, these same boys—now grown men—are expected to *express themselves* and *communicate their feelings*. Oh, so NOW you want them to talk? After a lifetime of hearing *"Crying is for the weak"* and *"Toughen up, bro"*? Yeah, no. That ship sank a long time ago, my friend. So now, instead of admitting they're sad, they just randomly fix things that aren't broken, like standing in front of the fridge muttering, *"Yeah, I was just thinking maybe the door could open… smoother."* Or they watch sports with the emotional intensity of a Shakespearean tragedy, gripping their beer can tighter every time their team loses, muttering *"I'm fine. TOTALLY fine."* Or they drop the most emotionally charged statement ever—*"It is what it is"*—as if it's some sort of ancient wisdom instead of a cry for help.

And the worst part? When they *do* finally hit a breaking point, people have the *audacity* to be surprised. Like, *"Wow, I had no idea he was struggling."* NO KIDDING. He tried to tell you when he was six, and you told him to *walk it off!* Listen, feminism means **equality.** Not just for women, but for *everyone.* That includes giving men the basic human right to *feel things* without being shamed for it. You wanna empower women? Great. But maybe let's also stop raising men to think their only emotions should be **anger, indifference, or gym.** Let's normalize telling our sons *"It's okay to be sad."* Let's raise boys who know that their worth isn't measured by how "tough" they are, and that real strength isn't about hiding pain—it's about **facing it.**

But here's the thing: *just because you joke about it doesn't mean it's not serious.* It's okay to feel things deeply. It's okay to have bad days (or bad weeks… or months… you get the point). You're not "too sensitive." You're not "just overthinking." You're literally a human trying to figure out life, and honestly? That's already hard enough without pretending you're fine all the time.

CHAPTER-5

Turning 18: Where's the User Manual?

So, I'm turning 18 in July. Officially legal. Supposedly grown-up. The world expects me to start making *wise* life choices, but I still take 20 minutes to decide what to order at a restaurant. I mean, how am I supposed to pick a *career* when I can't even commit to a Netflix show without second-guessing?

And the worst part? I've *seen* what happens next. My close ones—the ones who turned 18 before me—went in all excited, like, *"Yay, adulthood!"* ...only to realize **this whole thing is one giant scam.**

See, they told us that turning 18 means independence, freedom, and *finally* being taken seriously. What they *didn't* tell us is that it also means panic attacks over the future, the sudden need to understand taxes (what even *are* those?), and an unshakable feeling that **everyone else is moving forward while you're still buffering.**

Choosing "The Right Path" (Or Just Guessing and Hoping for the Best)

The moment you hit 18, there's this unspoken rule that you need to have a *solid* life plan. What do you want to study? Where do you want to work? Where do you see yourself in five years?

Excuse me, I don't even know what I'm eating for lunch tomorrow, and you want me to predict my *entire existence*?

Yet, somehow, society expects us to pull out a roadmap of our future like we've had it figured out since birth. *"Oh yes, I've always known I'd be a successful lawyer, marry at 27, buy a house at 30, and retire early."* Like, no. The real answer is: *I don't know, but I'm hoping I figure it out before my WiFi bill is due.*

But I get it. The pressure is real. I've watched my friends go through this existential crisis, pretending they have a grand plan while secretly spiralling. There's the cousin who was dead set on engineering—until he actually *did* engineering and realized he'd rather build LEGO than design circuits. Then there's my friend who *swore* she'd study abroad, only to change her mind last minute because, surprise surprise, life is *hella* expensive. And, of course, the classic category—relationships. Those who thought they found their *forever* only to realize that dating as an adult is basically just filling out an application for future heartbreak.

"But You Must Have Some Plan?" (Sure, Let Me Just Make One Up Real Quick)

The funny thing is, if you *don't* have a concrete answer to these life questions, people look at you like you just said you believe the Earth is flat.

"Oh, you're still deciding?"

"Beta, you should have some direction by now."

"You're wasting your time!"

Wasting *what* time? I'm 18, not 80. I still have time to mess up, change my mind, and rethink my choices at least *ten more times*. I mean, if 40-year-olds can switch careers, why am I expected to *lock down my entire fate* before I've even mastered boiling an egg?

But no, apparently, by 18, you must be either:

A doctor
An engineer
A scientist
A disappointment

(And no, I refuse to believe there are other options in Indian households.)

So, we panic. We start picking things randomly, hoping something sticks. One day you're thinking about being a journalist, the next day a psychologist, and by the end of the week, you've somehow convinced yourself that marine biology *might* be your calling (despite living nowhere near the ocean).

And the truth is? That's okay. *Nobody actually knows what they're doing.* Some just look more confident while winging it.

The Myth of "Figuring It All Out"

There's a moment when you realize that all those *"adults"* you looked up to when you were younger? Yeah, they were faking it too.

I used to think that by the time you reached your 20s, you'd have it all together—steady career, stable life, wisdom pouring out of your pores. You know, waking up at 6 AM, drinking black coffee without making *that* face, and investing in stocks like a responsible grown-up. But now? I see my seniors panicking over job applications, switching careers like outfit changes, and realizing that adulting is just *controlled chaos with better PR.*

Like take my cousin, for example. The same guy who spent all of last year giving TED-Talk-level speeches about *"following your passion"*? Yeah, last week, he texted me, *"Bro, I don't even know what my passion IS."* Sir, WHAT? You just made me feel guilty for not having my *five-year plan* ready while you were out here *vibing* with uncertainty the whole time??

And then there's my other cousin—Mr. *"Financial Stability Is Key."* Talks about investments like he's Warren Buffett, keeps saying things like *"It's not about how much you earn, it's about how much you save."* Very inspiring. Except, every month, I see him dramatically sighing at his credit card bill like it personally betrayed him.

See? **Nobody actually knows what they're doing.** They just act like they do. It's like a giant episode of *"Who's the Best at Pretending?"* and I refuse to believe anyone is winning.

Another thing I've noticed? The sheer amount of times people switch career paths like it's a game of musical chairs.

One of my seniors was convinced he was destined to be a software engineer. He even made a *LinkedIn* post about how coding was his *"true calling."* Fast forward six months? He's now doing an MBA and refuses to even look at a JavaScript file. *"Coding is a scam,"* he told me, *"I'm never touching it again."* The betrayal.

Then there's my friend who was *obsessed* with becoming a psychologist. She read psychology books for *fun* (I know, concerning). She even said things like *"I love understanding the human mind"* with a sparkle in her eye. A year into her degree? *"I hate people."* Ma'am, WHAT happened??

And don't even get me started on the *"I'll take a drop year to figure things out"* squad. One year turns into two, and suddenly, they're trying to convince everyone (including themselves) that *"experience is more valuable than a degree."*

Basically, career crises are just a personality trait at this point.

The Art of "Acting Mature" While Lowkey Falling Apart

Another thing about turning 18+? Apparently, you have to start *"acting mature."* Which—um, excuse me—**what does that even mean???**

Like, am I supposed to wake up one day and suddenly **love** grocery shopping? Am I meant to develop a deep, emotional connection with a well-organized spice rack? Should I automatically understand what *mutual funds* are, or will a *PDF mysteriously appear in my brain* explaining how taxes work?

Because, let me tell you, I still have to double-check the cooking time for *basic rice* every single time I make it. And don't even get me started on the internal breakdown I have every time I have to book an appointment over the phone.

And yet, I look around and see people my age *faking* adulthood so well. Like my friend—who, I swear, was the most childish person in existence—suddenly started talking about *"building assets"* and *"long-term investments."* I had to pause for a second. Sir, weren't you the same person who spent **45 minutes** trying to decide between pani puri or aloo tikki??? NOW YOU'RE OUT HERE MAKING **FINANCIAL DECISIONS???**

Meanwhile, I'm still getting my mother to fill out forms for me because, honestly? I trust her handwriting more than I trust my life choices. I mean, let's be real—have you ever tried filling out a government form? One spelling mistake, and suddenly, your entire identity is under investigation.

But the real kicker? The biggest scam of adulthood?

Nobody actually feels like an adult.

Some people are out here getting married, having kids, and making *actual* responsible choices, while I still panic over whether *"Regards"* in an email makes me sound too robotic, but *"Best"* makes me sound fake.

And let's not forget the **phone call crisis.** You know the one. The minute someone says *"Could you call and confirm?"* my soul *leaves* my body. Like, what do you mean *CALL*? Can't I just send an email and pretend I don't exist??

At this point, I'm convinced that being an adult isn't about *actually* knowing things. It's just about **pretending like you do**—with a slightly more expensive skincare routine.

Why It Feels Like Everyone Else is Speeding Through Life While You're Stuck in Traffic

Ah yes, my personal favorite existential crisis—the illusion that everyone else is miles ahead of you while you're stuck waiting for life to load like a bad WiFi connection.

You open Instagram, and BAM—someone's moving to a new country, casually posting airport selfies with *"On to new adventures "* in the caption. Someone else just landed a six-figure job at a fancy-sounding company you've never even heard of, and their LinkedIn is practically glowing. Another person is getting engaged, complete with a *4K drone-shot* proposal video that looks straight out of a Bollywood movie.

And you? You're sitting on your bed, wrapped in a blanket like a human burrito, contemplating whether eating Maggi for the third time this week makes you a culinary genius or a cautionary tale.

But wait, it gets worse. Because not only does social media shove everyone's *highlight reel* in your face, but your *real-life* interactions don't help either.

You go to a family gathering, and the interrogation begins:

"Beta, what are your future plans?"

Me: *To survive.*

"Arre, but what are you DOING these days?"

Me: *My best.*

"You know, Sharma ji's son just bought a house in Canada. And you?"

Me: *Considering blocking you, Aunty.*

I've watched my close ones spiral into this *"am I behind?"* panic too. It doesn't matter what stage of life they're in—18, 22, 25—there's always someone who seems to be doing "better." One friend landed her *dream job* right after college, but she still lies awake at night wondering if she's "successful enough." Another friend is in a *super cute* relationship, but every time he sees someone flexing their *solo backpacking in Europe* adventure, he starts questioning if he's *"missing out."*

It. Never. Ends.

But here's the scam—there is **no** fixed timeline. Life isn't a one-size-fits-all schedule where everyone gets handed a checklist:

Graduate at 21
Get a high-paying job by 23
Fall in love by 25
Buy a house by 28
Unlock inner peace by 30

NO. That's not how it works. Some people peak early, some people peak late, and some of us? We're still buffering.

The people who seem ahead? They might not be as happy as they look. The ones who seem lost? They might find their way later. And the *real plot twist*? Everyone—**literally everyone**—is confused. Some just hide it behind aesthetic Instagram stories and corporate-sounding job titles.

So the next time it feels like life is a highway and you're the only one stuck at a red light, remember: **some people are driving in circles, some are taking detours, and some are just pretending they know the way.**

And if all else fails? Just put on your seatbelt, blast your favorite song, and enjoy the ride.

Final Thoughts (Not That I Have It All Figured Out Either)

So, yeah. In a few months, I'll be 18, stepping into this wild mess of "adulthood." And if there's one thing I've learned from watching my close ones go through it, it's this:

Nobody has a clue.
Everybody is winging it.
It's okay to be lost.

Adulthood isn't about having all the answers—it's about getting comfortable with *not* having them. And if that means making a few wrong turns, eating way too much comfort food, and occasionally screaming into a pillow, then hey—sign me up.

CHAPTER-6

"Life's Deadline? Didn't Get the Memo."

Turning 18 in July, and honestly? I'm scared. Not because of adulthood itself, but because I've seen what comes next—the endless pressure of sticking to the timeline. Ah, the great cosmic rulebook that nobody wrote, yet somehow everyone follows. You know the one:

Graduate by 21
Land a dream job by 22
Be financially stable (whatever that means) by 25
Get married by 26
Own a house by 28
Have life completely figured out by 30

And if you dare to fall even slightly behind? People start looking at you like you're a glitch in the system.

It's like society decided that life is some strictly timed, perfectly planned assembly line. One delay, and suddenly, there's an existential crisis knocking at your door.

I know people who are 23 and already panicking because they don't have a six-figure salary, a luxury apartment, and a partner who looks like they walked straight out of a romantic novel. Meanwhile, I'm over here struggling to convince myself that having cereal for dinner isn't a personality trait.

But let's be honest—who even decided these deadlines?

Because the more I look around, the more I realize that nobody's actually following this so-called timeline.

Someone I know spent years pursuing a degree, only to realize they hated that field and switched careers completely at 30. Another got married at 24, divorced at 26, and is now happier than ever. A friend took a gap year because burnout is real, and guess what? The world didn't end.

And yet, despite all this proof that life isn't a race, there's still this overwhelming pressure to keep moving, to constantly prove that you're not falling behind.

We scroll through LinkedIn, see someone younger than us launching a startup, and suddenly, all our personal achievements feel like they belong in the discount aisle. We see someone from school buying a car while we're still figuring out how to split a pizza bill without using a calculator.

And the worst part? Burnout culture makes it even worse.

There's this bizarre obsession with being productive every waking second. If you're not constantly working, learning, networking, or side-hustling, are you even trying?

Can we all just pause for a second? Can we normalize taking a break without immediately labeling it as laziness?

Because, let's be real—this race never actually ends.

First, it's about getting into a good college. Then, it's about landing a good job. Then, it's about promotions. Then, marriage. Then, kids. Then, buying a house. Then, planning for retirement. And before you know it, you're 70, wondering why you spent your entire life chasing goals you didn't even set for yourself.

So maybe, just maybe, the real success isn't in keeping up with an imaginary timeline.

Maybe the real success is in figuring out your own pace, even if that means taking an afternoon nap in the middle of the week.

Life's Not a Race... But Why is Everyone Speeding Past Me?

Entering adulthood is getting terrifying, you know what scarier? Watching people around me act like they've cracked the code to life while I'm still out here struggling to decide what to have for breakfast.

And okay, I get it—this is just the beginning. Right now, the pressure is mostly about what to study, what career to pick, and whether I should feel guilty for still needing my parents to remind me about deadlines. But from what I've seen in my close ones, this feeling? This constant game of *"Am I behind?"* never really ends.

Right now, I see people picking colleges and degrees with the confidence of a stock market expert. *"Finance is my passion,"* they say. *"Medicine is my calling."* And I just sit there thinking—

since when did we all figure out our passions? Last week, I was passionate about getting eight hours of sleep. The week before that, I was passionate about quitting everything and opening a book café. The week before *that*, I thought law was my dream. So, forgive me if I'm a little skeptical about people acting like they have a 20-year plan at 18.

And it doesn't stop there. Fast forward a few years, and suddenly, the milestones get even bigger.

By the time I'm 22, people will be graduating, getting degrees, and securing jobs that sound so fancy, you need a dictionary to understand what they do. *"I work in corporate risk assessment management with data-driven strategic analysis."* Bro, what? I just learned how to fill out a tax form.

By 25, it's the real Hunger Games. Some people will be launching businesses, some will be buying houses, and some will be getting *married.* MARRIED. I still have a crisis when I have to pick a new shampoo, and people will be out here choosing life partners?

And then, somewhere between 26 and 30, it turns into a full-blown *achievement Olympics.* Promotions, new investments, "self-made" success stories. Meanwhile, I already know I'm going to be sitting there, refreshing LinkedIn like it's a reality TV show and wondering if I should start manifesting wealth or just accept my fate.

But here's the part nobody tells you—*even the ones who seem ahead aren't actually ahead.* I've seen it happen. The people who look the most "sorted" right now? Some of them are already second-guessing everything. The ones who took their time? They're finding their own way at their own pace. There is no *one* timeline, just a bunch of people pretending they've got everything under control.

And let's talk about social media, the biggest scam of all. By the time I'm 23, my feed is probably going to be a never-ending highlight reel of people "thriving." Someone posting about their *dream job*, someone else announcing their engagement, another person casually vacationing in Santorini like it's a weekend getaway. And me? Sitting there in my pajamas, aggressively Googling *"How do I stop comparing myself to people who look more successful than me?"*

Because that's what this whole thing is, right? One big comparison game. The second you start to feel okay about where you are, you see someone else achieving something, and suddenly, you feel like you're *behind.* But behind *what* exactly? There's no universal success deadline. Some people peak early, some peak later, some take detours, and some change their entire direction halfway through.

Honestly, I already know I'm going to struggle with this in the future. I'll probably have moments where I stare at other people's lives and think, *"Should I be doing more?"* But if there's one thing I've learned from watching my close ones, it's that *nobody actually knows what they're doing.* Some people are just better at looking like they do.

So yeah, maybe in a few years, I'll be sitting at 25, watching people announce their big life changes and feeling that little voice creep in saying, *"You're falling behind."* But I hope that future me will also remember this—**life isn't a race, and if it is, we're all just running in different directions anyway.**

At some point in the near future, I just know I'm going to wake up, scroll through my phone, and be greeted by yet another motivational post that says something like:

"You have the same 24 hours as Elon Musk. Use them wisely."

And that's the exact moment I will throw my phone across the room and go back to sleep.

Because let's be real—do I actually have the same 24 hours as billionaires with personal assistants, private jets, and people who cook their meals for them? No. I have the same 24 hours as a sleep-deprived, anxiety-ridden 20-something-year-old who's trying to figure out whether drinking another cup of coffee is self-care or self-destruction.

But here's the thing—this whole *"every second of your life must be productive"* mindset? It's the biggest scam of adulthood.

I've already seen people around me fall for it. One minute, they're normal humans with hobbies and free time, and the next, they're obsessively reading *self-improvement* books and tracking their screen time like it's a stock market graph. Suddenly, if you're not waking up at 5 AM, journaling, hitting the gym, working 10 hours a day, AND running a side hustle, you're *wasting your potential.*

Like, bro. Let me breathe.

And this is where burnout sneaks in like a villain in a thriller movie—slow at first, but by the time you realize it's there, you're already mentally and physically exhausted. One second you're *grinding* through life, and the next, you're lying on the floor, questioning your entire existence, wondering if the mitochondria really *is* the powerhouse of the cell, or if that was just the first of many lies we were fed.

I've seen it happen. People go all in, working like robots, until one day, they just… crash. They start feeling guilty for resting, for taking a break, for not turning every second of their life into a *"hustle."* And the worst part? Society celebrates burnout as if it's an *achievement.*

"Oh, you only sleep 4 hours a night? Wow, so dedicated!"
"You haven't taken a vacation in 3 years? That's true commitment!"
"You work through your lunch breaks? That's what winners do!"

No, that's what *tired* people do. That's what *miserable* people do. That's what people do when they've been tricked into thinking that their *entire worth is based on how much they produce.*

And the funniest part? The *race* never actually ends.

You think once you land a good job, you'll finally *relax*? Nope. Now you have to work harder to get promoted. You think once you hit a certain salary, you'll finally *be happy*? Nope. Now you have to keep pushing to *maintain* that lifestyle. You think once you reach a certain level of success, you'll finally *feel fulfilled*? Nope. Because society will just move the goalpost again and tell you that *true* success means something *even bigger.*

The whole system is built to make you feel like you're *always* behind, like you *always* have to be doing more. And if you're not? If you decide to just… exist, enjoy life, maybe take a nap at 2 PM for no reason? Suddenly, you're *lazy*. You're *unmotivated*. You're *not living up to your potential*.

And honestly? That's exhausting.

So, future me, if you're reading this and you're feeling like you're *not doing enough*, just remember—**success isn't just about how busy you are. It's about whether you're actually happy.** And if that means taking a break, ignoring hustle culture, and just living life at your own pace? Then congrats. You've already won the game that everyone else is too.

CHAPTER-7

Dad, I Promise It's Not a Rebel Speech – Just Hear Me Out!

I have a therapist.

Her name is Dr. Doom, and she didn't exactly come with a degree or a referral. One day, she just showed up in my mind, uninvited, like an unholy mix of an overly critical parent and a judgmental best friend. And like any unwanted guest, she took up way too much space and started talking. All the time. Whether I wanted it or not.

Dr. Doom's therapy sessions are *not* what you'd expect from a traditional therapist. She doesn't say, "Tell me how that makes you feel." No, her sessions are more like random critiques, usually delivered in the most inconvenient moments, like when I'm about to fall asleep, or in the middle of a conversation when I'm trying to focus.

Her voice is loud, intrusive, and completely unhelpful. She likes to start with lines like:

"You should've been a lawyer by now. Too bad you took the easy way out."

"Teaching? Really? You're going to *settle* for teaching?"

She never lets me forget how much I'm *failing* to meet the lofty expectations I set for myself when I was younger.

See, I used to dream about being a lawyer. Not just any lawyer, but a *kick-ass* lawyer. One who stands up for the people who can't speak for themselves, who stands in the courtroom with confidence, and who wins cases with an argument so tight, it could break glass. I imagined myself wearing a suit (obviously, dramatic flair was involved), delivering powerful speeches, and having my name associated with landmark cases. The kind of lawyer you see on TV in the legal dramas where people clap and say, "She's brilliant!"

But the road to that dream wasn't as clear as I'd hoped.

And then there were the voices of well-meaning relatives, who didn't have the same vision for me. They were quick to offer their "advice," always with the best of intentions, but it always felt like they were drawing a map to a future I didn't want.

"A lawyer? For a girl? That's a tough path. You'll have to sacrifice everything."

"Why not teach? It's safer. Steady income. Good life. You'll be happy."

And at the time, I didn't know how to fight against those opinions. I folded. I made the decision to pursue teaching, even though it wasn't my first choice. And at first, I thought it would be a temporary thing. Something to do while I figured out how to get to law school. But as I dove deeper into it, I realized something—teaching wasn't just "something to do." I actually loved it. It felt right in so many ways.

But Dr. Doom didn't see it that way. She just kept ranting about how I was "wasting" my potential. She would pop up at the most random times, practically screaming at me:

"What are you doing? Teaching isn't going to make you a lawyer. You're never going to get there."

And I'd feel that doubt creeping in, the nagging feeling that maybe she was right. Maybe I *had* given up. Maybe I wasn't cut out for the law I had dreamed of all those years.

But here's the thing—teaching *isn't* a pit stop. I realized that. It's not a consolation prize for failing at law. It's something I can love, something that makes a difference in my own way. I'm shaping minds, helping students grow. It's meaningful work, and I don't take that lightly.

But just because I love teaching doesn't mean it's where I'm going to stay forever. I have bigger dreams, dreams that are still in motion.

The thing is, I'm not abandoning law. I'm *redefining* it. I'm starting with a big first step, the one that's going to launch me toward everything I've ever wanted to do. And yes, that step involves going abroad to pursue my bachelor's in education.

At first, I was hesitant. Teaching wasn't the end goal, but it *is* the first step in a longer journey. I could feel Dr. Doom's voice getting louder, her doubts clawing at me again. "You're making a mistake," she'd hiss. "You're just postponing your dreams."

But here's the thing—this isn't a detour. It's the first step to creating a foundation for the life I want. I'm going to study abroad, get my degree in education, and carve out a life in a completely new place, all while preparing for the next chapter: law.

And once I've built that foundation—once I've settled into my new life, carved out my career, and have experienced everything that studying abroad has to offer—I'll go to law school. I'm not giving up on that dream, but I've learned that I don't have to rush. Life isn't a race, and maybe that's where Dr. Doom's biggest mistake is—she thinks I'm racing against something, when I'm simply walking at my own pace, letting life unfold.

So, while Dr. Doom still has a lot to say, I'm learning how to ignore her more. Her words are just background noise now. The real plan is clear, and it starts with studying abroad for my bachelor's in education.

The excitement of being in a new place, meeting new people, exploring a whole new culture—it's all coming together. And eventually, once I've built a life, once I've done the work and settled into the rhythm of my new world, I'll go back to my dreams. I'll go to law school and take that path. It'll just be on my terms, and on my time.

I've never been one to follow someone else's plan, especially not Dr. Doom's. And as much as she tries to remind me of what I *should* have done, I know that the journey I'm starting right now is exactly where I need to be. The rest will follow.

So let her yell. Let her criticize. But I'm finally listening to my own voice now. And it's saying: This is the first step.

So, here's the thing—I talk a lot. And by *a lot*, I mean I rarely leave a space where my thoughts aren't tumbling out of my mouth. Some days, it's like there's a non-stop parade of words inside my head, and my mouth just can't keep up. It's like an overactive tap that *never* stops flowing.

But, you know, there are some people who don't exactly love this about me. Especially my parents.

"You talk too much," they say, looking at me like I'm an overenthusiastic puppy who's just learned how to bark in 47 different tones. "Daneet, can you just *be quiet* for five minutes?" they'll ask, like I'm asking for the world when I ask for a tiny, little break to just, well, talk.

"Why don't you listen more and talk less?" my dad will say, running his hand through his hair, probably out of sheer frustration that he's been forced to listen to me for the past *hour*. My mom, with a sigh so dramatic it could win an Oscar, adds, "You've got the gift of gab, kiddo, but can you *not* use it so much?"

You know what? Sometimes I wonder if there's a hidden camera in our house. Like, *this* is the real-life sitcom, and I'm the quirky, talkative lead character with no off switch. The joke's on me. They love me, of course, but... *silence* is apparently a luxury in my home.

But here's the kicker—when I try to be quiet, when I make an effort to hold back my words... I can't. It's like trying to hold back a flood with a paper towel. I'll sit there, nodding in agreement, trying to be *normal*, trying to just blend in and keep it all in. But then, out it comes:

"But what about the fact that...?"

"I was thinking earlier, do you think...?"

"Wait, hold up, let me finish this thought!"

And my parents? They just look at each other and exchange the world's most exhausted sigh. It's as if they've been through this *so many times* they have their sighs pre-recorded.

But here's the thing—I've realized that I don't want to *stop*. Talking is just how I process life. It's how I figure out what I believe, how I build my world view. And yes, it gets a bit intense, sometimes. But isn't that just *me*?

At first, I thought I had to change this part of myself. The world is filled with people who stay quiet, who wait their turn to speak. I wanted to be "normal" for once. I thought, *maybe I'll become the quiet one. Maybe I'll just hold back, be like everyone else and not disrupt the silence.*

I tried that. I really did.

But then came the *epic* realization. I'm not built that way. I can't do silence. And I shouldn't have to.

I'm not here to play it safe. If I keep my mouth shut, I'll never reach my full potential. It's not even about impressing people or showing them how *smart* I am (because, let's be real, I'm not trying to compete with anyone). It's about being real. Being me. I'm unapologetically myself, even when my parents want me to just take a breath and be *normal* for five seconds.

And you know what? Maybe it's *their* problem. I mean, honestly, I've been listening to their stories my entire life. They've had their turn in the spotlight. Now, it's my time.

But deep down, I know they mean well. They want me to be successful, of course. They want me to "get somewhere." But success, for them, sometimes means blending in, not making waves, staying under the radar. For them, it's the calm, measured path. But for me? I'm not about to do that. I *need* to make waves. I need to shake things up. I want to break free from that mold, to do something different. And the first step is to find the balance between my enthusiasm and their desire for quiet.

Because I refuse to apologize for being loud. For being outspoken. For being me.

Sure, I'll keep hearing the "You talk too much" comments from my parents, and I'll probably always feel like I'm too much for them sometimes. But guess what? I'm learning to own it. I'm learning that talking too much doesn't make me less of a person. It doesn't make me *wrong*. In fact, maybe I talk too much because I'm passionate, because I'm excited to share my world with everyone. Is that really such a crime?

Now, I'm preparing to go abroad. It's the first step in a huge, exciting journey. Sure, I'm a little anxious. Sure, I'm leaving behind what's familiar. But I'm also filled with so much energy, so much potential, that I can't help but talk about it. I *need* to talk about it. This is the start of something new—something big—and I want everyone to know about it. I want to share my excitement, my fears, my dreams. I want to walk into the world with my head held high, talking loud enough for people to hear me, because if they don't... well, they'll miss out on some of the most important parts of me.

But you know, here's something I really, really want to say—especially to all the Indian parents out there: *Let your daughters talk.*

Seriously. Don't hush them. Don't silence their voices because you're scared they'll be too "loud" or "too much." The world, especially for women, is already a place where we're often told to stay quiet, to blend in, to be humble and small. But we don't have to be. If you let your daughters speak, if you encourage them to express their ideas, to argue their point, to share their thoughts freely... you're not just raising kids who can debate a point. You're raising future leaders who can stand their ground in a world that often wants to shut them up. You're giving them a tool that will carry them through life—how to speak up when it matters most, how to be confident in their voice, how to say, *I'm here, and I have something important to say.*

Indian parents, let your daughters find their voice. Let them use it. Let them be the loud, unapologetic force they're meant to be. The future is built on the voices that rise above the noise, not the ones that stay silent.

So, to all the people who tell me I talk too much, I say this: I'm not going to change who I am. I'm going to keep talking. I'm going to keep being outspoken. I'll keep being *me.* And if that's too much for some people to handle, well, that's their problem.

This world is built on voices. The quiet ones will be heard, sure, but the loud ones—the ones who speak up, who stand firm and refuse to shrink—those are the ones who create the future. And that's exactly what I plan to do. I'm going to create my future. On my terms. Outspoken, passionate, and unapologetic.

And I'll make it big.

Here's where things get a little deeper. I've been thinking a lot about my future—about the decisions I'm going to make, the choices that will shape the rest of my life. And, of course, when I think about it, my mind goes straight to the people who have been with me through it all: my parents. I love them. I respect them. I've always valued their guidance, their wisdom, their care. They've worked hard to give me the best of everything, and I'm forever grateful for that.

But here's the thing: as I step into the world, as I start making decisions for my future, I want them to understand something.

I want to make my own choices.

Yes, I know I'm still young, and yes, I've made mistakes. But every step, every failure, every disappointment has taught me something valuable. I don't want to go through life with a "safe" decision that's someone else's. I want to make my own decisions, even if I fail. Even if I face betrayal or get hurt. I want to know that whatever path I choose, I chose it with my own hands, my own heart.

I want to take control of my life—starting now, starting with the choices that matter most to me. Whether it's about where I live, what I work for, who I become, or what my future looks like.

At 21, I want to be working on my own ethics, shaping my own destiny. It's important to me that I own the decisions I make because, at the end of the day, this is *my* life. Not anyone else's.

I'm not asking for permission. I'm asking for understanding. And support. Because, yes, I will make mistakes. Yes, I'll stumble. But I will learn from them. I will rise, and I will build something that's *mine*. I want to take full ownership of my choices—whether it's a job, a degree, a relationship, or a goal I set. I need my parents to see that this isn't a rebellion. It's my journey.

And when I say I want to take my own decisions, this extends to my personal life too. I don't want to sound like I'm challenging the rules or rebelling against the values my family has given me, especially in an Indian household. I've seen how tough it can be to navigate personal choices when you're expected to follow the traditional path. But I know that I need to be independent. I need to find my own way, and for that, I need to get a job first, stand on my own feet, and then take decisions that align with who I am—without feeling the weight of everyone else's expectations on me.

It's not about rejecting everything that's been taught to me. It's about growing into the person I'm meant to be. It's about realizing that independence is not something to fear but something to celebrate. I want my parents to trust me, especially my dad. I want him to see that I'm capable of making decisions, both big and small, on my own. I want him to understand that while I respect the guidance he has always provided, I also need the freedom to step out and chart my own course.

So yes, I need their support now more than ever. I need them to step back, just a little, and trust that I can do this. That I will learn and grow, with or without their approval. But most importantly, I need them to know I respect them deeply, and that I love them. My choices might not always align with their vision for me, but they will always be made with love and respect for everything they've done to get me to this point.

It's time for me to figure out who I am on my own terms. I want to shape my life, not based on what I think they want for me, but on what feels true to me. I want to live without regrets, knowing that the decisions I make are mine.

And when I succeed? I want them to be there, proud, because they saw me take that leap. And when I fail? I want them to be there, supporting me, because they saw me fall but also rise again.

Someday, I will meet new people. I will build relationships. I will fall in love, and yes, I want to make those decisions too. But here's the thing I hope my dad knows: when that time comes, I want him to be the first person I turn to, to know about it, and to support me, just like he has always supported me through everything else. I don't want him to feel like I'm rebelling, I want him to feel proud that I'm learning how to navigate the world, how to make decisions that feel right to me.

It's a hard conversation to have. It feels a little *heavy*, honestly. But I hope they understand. Because this is not about rejecting them. It's about me finally finding my own wings.

So, here it is, plain and simple: I want to take my own decisions. I'm not asking for control. I'm asking for trust. And I need them to know that, at the end of the day, no matter what happens, I'll always love them and respect them. But it's time for me to decide.

As I think about the future, there's one thing I hope for above all else: I want to build a relationship with my dad that feels more like a friendship. I don't want to be the daughter who keeps everything to herself or feels like I can't share the important stuff with him. I want us to be able to sit down and talk, not just about the everyday things, but about life, my dreams, my challenges, and yes—even the boys I meet along the way. I want to be able to tell him about the ups and downs without holding back, knowing that I'll be heard, not judged.

I know it's not always easy, especially in a traditional setting where certain things are just not openly discussed. But that's why I'm hoping, with time, we can create that kind of bond. One where I can share the full picture of my life with him, from my career goals to my friendships and even my failures. I want him to see me as someone who is figuring things out, not someone who has everything perfectly mapped out. I want him to be there as I make mistakes and learn, as well as when I succeed.

When I'm 21 and standing on my own two feet with a job, I want to be able to come home and talk about the exciting parts of my day, the difficult decisions I'm making, and the people I meet. I want to be able to ask for advice when I need it, and just as importantly, I want to be able to share the small victories too. And yes, there will be times when I talk about the romantic side of life, the crushes, the love, the heartbreaks. I hope he'll be the first person I can talk to without feeling awkward or misunderstood.

I don't want to sound like I'm pushing boundaries just for the sake of it. I'm not looking to be rebellious or defy everything I've been taught. But I do want to feel free enough to express myself, to let my dad in on the real stuff. The kind of conversations that are full of honesty, humor, and trust. The kind that make us feel like we're more than just father and daughter—we're people, learning from each other.

At the end of the day, I want my dad to understand that this isn't about me stepping away or rejecting his influence. It's about me growing into the person I'm meant to be and wanting to do that with him by my side. I want him to know that, even when I'm taking control of my decisions and living life on my own terms, I'm still going to need him, just in a new way. I hope that, as time goes on, we'll both find a way to connect on a deeper level, where I'm not afraid to be myself around him.

Someday, when I'm making choices about my life, I want to look to him and feel that same sense of trust and support I've always felt. I hope we can laugh together, share the meaningful moments, and have conversations where we don't need to be anyone but ourselves. I'm not asking for anything extraordinary. Just a relationship where we both see each other as equals, with mutual respect and understanding. And, as I move forward with my life, I hope that's the kind of bond we can build—one that feels natural, one that will last.

CHAPTER-8

Chapter: *Emotional Baggage: Carry-On or Check-In?*

Imagine this: You're at the airport, dragging a suitcase that's clearly too heavy. You didn't pack light, but you *did* convince yourself you could handle it. Kind of like how we convince ourselves that we're carrying *no emotional baggage* whatsoever. "I'm fine," we say, grinning through it while dragging that emotional carry-on stuffed with everything from unspoken worries to childhood memories. Sure, it's not a full-sized suitcase, but it's filled with enough unresolved feelings to make you break into a cold sweat at the thought of actually *thinking* about it.

Here's the deal: emotions are like luggage. You can pretend they're not there, but eventually, they start spilling out. Maybe it's in the middle of a group hangout when you laugh a little too hard at a joke that hits *too close to home.* Maybe it's that one friend who's trying to have a serious conversation, and you can't stop shifting uncomfortably in your seat. The baggage is real, my friend.

"Denial is like Tetris for the emotionally incompetent. You think you've packed it all in, but one piece is about to pop out, and it's going to be awkward." – Me, probably while trying to ignore my emotional baggage at the dinner table.

You know that feeling when you say, "I'm just tired," but we both know that's a *lie*? You're not just tired—you're emotionally drained, mentally exhausted, and possibly just one awkward social interaction away from falling apart. Suppression is like an invisibility cloak for your feelings. "Nothing's wrong," you tell yourself, as you shove another emotion into that imaginary suitcase. "It's fine."

But *is* it fine? Is it really? No, it's not. But we love to pretend it is, because facing your feelings sounds like too much work. Like, *why* would you want to confront that low-key resentment you've been carrying since your best friend borrowed your hoodie for the 42nd time? Or that embarrassment from the time you accidentally made a joke that fell flat in front of the group? It's way easier to just say, "I'm fine," and shove it all back into the emotional luggage. But guess what? Eventually, those suitcases get heavy. And you're the one dragging them around.

"Suppressing your emotions is like trying to fit too much junk in your closet. You know it's going to spill out when you least expect it." – Me, probably trying to ignore my feelings by binge-watching Netflix.

Let's talk about trauma. It's not a special edition item that deserves a pedestal. It's more like that weird souvenir you get at a theme park that you *never asked for* but somehow ends up on your shelf for years. "Oh, it wasn't that bad," we tell ourselves. But deep down, we know we've been emotionally dragging that souvenir around, pretending it doesn't exist, while it *silently* collects dust in the corner of our mind.

We joke about our traumas, don't we? "Haha, remember that time I cried over a math test? Good times." But in all honesty, laughing about something doesn't mean it's not affecting you. It's like trying to pretend you don't feel that sinking feeling when you see a message from your friend and you're worried about how they're doing. It's all that emotional baggage we *say* we've left behind—but somehow, it follows us around like that one person who keeps sending you *all* the memes.

"Trauma is like that one questionable meme your friend sends you that you can't unsee. It's not funny, and it never really goes away." – Me, probably contemplating my existence after scrolling through Twitter at 2 AM.

Now, let's get real. We all have that one friend who's got *a lot* going on under the surface, but instead of talking it out, they just keep shoving it all under the rug—until one day, they start walking on that rug, and it trips them up. Let me tell you about a friend of mine, who we'll call *"Neha"* (for privacy reasons, of course). We used to be close, but over time, things started changing. She used to be insecure, and I could tell—those little jabs, passive-aggressive comments that seemed innocent at first, but they really piled up. Like when she'd say, "I don't know why you're so confident, it's a bit much," or when she'd do her best to criticize my every decision like it was *her* job. She didn't know boundaries.

At first, I was like, "Okay, maybe she's just joking." But as time went on, it wasn't funny anymore. It started to feel like every conversation we had was some subtle way of her putting me down. I found myself constantly walking on eggshells, making sure I didn't upset her. But honestly, I was *tired.* And then came the moment that no one saw coming: the *betrayal.* She went behind my back and spread rumors—things I'd confided in her, things that were personal, became gossip. The emotional toll? Not fun.

I confronted her about it, but instead of an apology, she got defensive, making it seem like I was overreacting. Classic, right? The "I'm fine" response. The one where you're trying to stay calm, but inside, you're just waiting to explode. We all know the feeling. I should have set boundaries earlier, but hey, emotional baggage is a real thing, and sometimes we don't even realize how heavy it's getting until we *can't* carry it anymore.

Boundaries – The Art of Saying 'No, You Can't' Without Feeling Like the World's Worst Person

So, let's talk about boundaries. You know, that word we all throw around like it's an Instagram hashtag. #Boundaries. But for some reason, no one ever tells you exactly how to set them. It's like you're supposed to just *know*, right? Like there's some secret boundary-setting manual hidden under a pile of self-help books. Spoiler: There's no manual, and you're the one who has to make the rules.

But here's the thing: Boundaries are not just about saying "No" to that one friend who texts you at 3 AM asking if you've seen the new Netflix show (you haven't, because you have a life, thank you very much). No, boundaries are about saying "No" to everything and everyone in your life that's slowly making you feel like you're drowning in their emotional baggage, while they casually sip their iced coffee and complain about their *first-world problems*.

Step 1: The 'No' Revolution

Let's be real. "No" is probably the hardest word in the English language. And not in that romantic, Shakespearean "Oh, how I doth love thee!" kind of way. No, in the "Why does saying no make me feel like I'm a horrible person?" kind of way. And don't even get me started on the guilt that follows. You say "No" once, and suddenly you feel like you've committed some grave moral offense, like you just kicked a puppy and ate its sandwich. I mean, who knew setting boundaries would feel like you're playing emotional Jenga and you're one piece away from the tower toppling over?

But here's the secret: *No* is actually a form of self-love, not selfishness. It's the emotional equivalent of locking your phone screen when your annoying group chat starts blowing up. Just because your friends (or *cough* frenemies) want you to jump in and take care of their problems does not mean you need to drop everything and become their unpaid emotional therapist. Boundaries are your way of saying, "Nope, not today, Satan." And guess what? That's okay.

Step 2: Setting Boundaries, Not Building Fortresses

Now, let's clear something up. Setting boundaries doesn't mean you're building a wall so high that no one can ever get in. If that was the case, we'd all be living in emotional Fort Knox, and that would be... well, honestly kind of awesome, but also extremely isolating. Boundaries are more like... *guardrails*—keeping you from falling off the emotional cliff, but still allowing people to visit without driving you into a state of permanent burn-out.

Think of it like this: Boundaries are like when your friend asks if they can borrow your phone charger, and you respond with, "Sure, but I need it back in 30 minutes because I'm literally surviving on 4% battery, and if you take my charger, I might not make it to tomorrow."

It's not a fortress. It's a polite, yet firm *boundary* that says, "I'm here for you, but my time, energy, and emotional space are not infinite."

"Boundaries are like WiFi passwords—once they're in place, people respect them. But if you don't set them, don't be surprised when everyone's freeloading off your emotional bandwidth." — Me, probably finally figuring out how to get people to stop texting me at 1 AM.

Step 3: The Fear of Being the 'Bad Guy'

Now, here's where it gets tricky: the fear of being labeled *that* person—the bad guy. The one who says no, the one who's too selfish, too self-centered. This is where the real fun begins. Let me ask you this: Have you ever felt like saying no made you feel like you were going to be excommunicated from the entire friend group? It's like everyone's waiting for you to be the nice one, the "I'll do anything for you!" person, but the minute you say "No, I'm going to have a mental health day," suddenly you're the villain. You've just become the Grinch of Friendships.

News flash: Saying "No" doesn't make you the bad guy. In fact, it makes you a *hero*—the unsung hero who didn't let themselves drown in other people's emotional chaos. You're like the person at the party who quietly takes their coat and leaves before it turns into a chaotic disaster. You're saving your energy, and that's a *good thing.*

"Boundaries are like the 'Do Not Disturb' sign on your door. It doesn't mean you hate your friends. It just means you don't want to be

interrupted while you're trying to enjoy some peace and quiet... or, you know, avoid a mental breakdown." — Me, probably contemplating the meaning of life while hiding from a group chat.

Step 4: The Consequences of Not Setting Boundaries

Now, let's talk consequences. Not setting boundaries is like constantly lending your charger to people who *never* give it back. You end up drained, literally and figuratively. It's like this: You say yes to everything—yes to every request, every favor, every random question about the new season of *Stranger Things*—until one day, you realize you're running on empty and can barely function. Meanwhile, your "friends" have plugged themselves into your emotional charger without asking, and you're left with 1% of yourself, desperately hoping no one asks you to do anything else.

When you don't set boundaries, you become the emotional ATM. Everyone's coming to withdraw their stuff, but no one's depositing any emotional currency back into your account. And surprise, surprise, your emotional balance hits negative, and you're suddenly the one who feels bad when you have to say no.

"Not setting boundaries is like going to a party without checking the snack table first. You're doing fine until you realize you've been handing out chips and dips to everyone else, and now there's nothing left for you. Who's the real loser here?" — Me, probably eyeing my emotional snack supply and realizing I've given it all away.

Step 5: The Liberation of 'No'

And here's the ultimate *mic drop* moment: the *liberation of 'No.'* Saying no isn't just about protecting your time and energy—it's about taking back control of your life. It's like going on a shopping spree and saying, "No, I don't want that toxic relationship. No, I don't want that guilt trip." You get to decide what stays, what goes, and what gets to park its emotional baggage at your front door.

Setting boundaries doesn't mean being a robot. It doesn't mean you're some cold, heartless person. It just means that you respect yourself enough to put your needs first. And believe me, there's nothing selfish about that. It's not only about protecting your sanity—it's also about preserving the quality of your relationships. When people know your boundaries, they're more likely to respect you, even if they occasionally give you a dramatic "OMG, you're being *so* selfish" face. *Newsflash*: It's not selfish to protect your mental health. It's self-preservation.

"Boundaries are your VIP pass to a drama-free life. Don't let anyone make you feel guilty for saying, 'No thanks, I'm good.'" — Me, probably finally achieving inner peace after blocking the 45th 'Hey, can I ask you something?' text of the day.

Final Thoughts:

Boundaries are a life skill. And while we're all stumbling through this maze of adulthood (or whatever phase of life this is), setting boundaries is like finding the one thing that will keep your emotional world from crashing down like a bad soap opera. They help you keep your energy intact, your peace of mind undisturbed, and your sanity from going on a permanent vacation. So, go ahead—set some boundaries, say "No" without feeling like you've just destroyed your entire social life, and *own* your peace.

After all, your happiness is your responsibility. Not anyone else's.

You know how when you're at the airport and your suitcase is just a bit over the weight limit, and they *still* charge you extra fees? Yeah, that's your mental health when you've been carting around emotional baggage for too long. You start thinking everything's fine, until one small inconvenience hits you, and suddenly you're like, "Wait, why am I crying over spilled milk? Oh right, it's because I've been ignoring all my feelings for the last year."

Mental health isn't a vacation, and neither is dealing with your emotions. The extra baggage fees? They come in the form of stress, anxiety, burnout, and the occasional random panic attack. And it's not the fun kind of anxiety where you get jittery before a big event. It's the kind that sneaks up on you like an old friend who hasn't paid back that *one* thing they borrowed two years ago.

"Ignoring your mental health is like leaving your luggage unattended. Eventually, someone's going to rummage through it and make you deal with it." – Me, probably staring at my reflection while wishing my emotional baggage could just disappear.

Alright, it's time to unpack. I know, it sounds *terrible*, but here's the thing: You can't avoid the emotional baggage forever. Unpacking your feelings, setting boundaries, and dealing with your past isn't something that can be done in one afternoon. It's like organizing your closet. You think you'll spend 10 minutes on it, but two hours later, you've discovered five missing socks, an old sweater you thought was lost, and a *lot* of dust.

But the cool part? The more you unpack, the lighter you feel. You can start letting go of what doesn't serve you anymore. And eventually, when someone asks you how you're doing, you can smile and actually mean it. Because your emotional luggage won't weigh you down anymore. You'll just be carrying around what you need—and hopefully, a few less unwanted souvenirs.

"Unpacking your emotions is like clearing out the junk drawer. It's messy, but it's so worth it when it's done." – Me, probably celebrating the fact that I finally dealt with my emotional clutter.

CHAPTER-9

If Love's the Destination, Can I See the Refund Policy First?

So everyone says the next phase is *the dream.*
Fall in love. Get married. Maybe to the person who once sent you "good night" texts with 17 emojis and an oddly threatening heart gif. Buy a house, raise a family, wake up to the smell of fresh coffee, baby giggles, and shared toothpaste.

Cute, right?

Yeah, sure. Until you zoom in and realize that a lot of those baby giggles come with sleepless nights, and that shared toothpaste is now the reason for your third argument this week. Because apparently "you never squeeze it from the bottom, RAVI!"

I'm still a teen, so technically I'm not there yet. But I'm watching. Closely. Like a Netflix crime doc narrator. Because when I look around, I don't see flawless fairy tales. I see something much messier. Something real.

I see parents who are so tired, they're running on caffeine and autopilot. I see couples who loved each other so much once, now barely making eye contact over dinner. I see people my age hiding their relationships like they're preparing for a secret mission. And honestly, the whole thing looks exhausting.

I see families that are held together by group texts and shared Wi-Fi passwords. And I see kids—tiny, sensitive, beautiful souls—asking for emotional attention from adults who were never taught how to emotionally attend to *themselves.*

And I wonder.

If love is supposed to save us… why does it sometimes feel like it's what we need saving from?

It's not the idea of love that's the issue. Love is warm. Love is home. Love is telling someone, "I know you're overwhelmed, but I believe in you anyway."

But real-life love?
It comes with extra toppings. Like ego. And stress. And differing ideas of "what's for dinner." You don't just marry a

person. You marry their entire Google Calendar, family WhatsApp group, past heartbreaks, and the fact that they don't believe in using coasters.

And parenting? Whew.

It's a full-time job disguised as a blessing.

I've seen parents stressed over school fees, screen time, career compromises, and their own identity, trying to hold it all together while their coffee gets cold for the sixth time that morning.

Some are genuinely doing their best. Some are just trying to survive the week.

Either way, the kids are watching. Just like I am. And some of us are quietly promising ourselves we'll do it differently—if we ever choose to do it at all.

Marriage sounds like stability, but sometimes it's just two people trying to remember why they liked each other in the first place. Divorce isn't always a tragedy anymore—sometimes it's just the next honest chapter.

But what do I know? I still Google how to boil pasta.

Still, it makes me think.

What if, one day, I fall in love? What if I want to marry him? What if I want to tell my parents that this loud, laugh-too-hard, chocolate-hating human is the one I choose?

Will I have the courage to say it out loud?

Honestly, probably not. I'll probably faint dramatically, wake up, and text it instead.

Or maybe I'll write an essay. "Dear Mom & Dad, this is a pre-booked emotional rollercoaster. Buckle up. Love, your daughter with excellent taste in humans."

But here's the thing.

I don't hate love. I don't fear adulthood. I just don't romanticize them blindly.

I don't want a Pinterest-perfect life with aesthetic babies and latte art. I want the real thing. I want a relationship where we can cry in the car together, not just pose in the car for stories. I want a family where kids feel safe, not silenced.

And I want to grow into a person who chooses love with her eyes wide open, not because it's expected—but because it's honest.

So maybe one day I will fall. Hard. Madly. Spotify-playlist-level in love.

But before I do, I want to rise. I want to rise into a person who knows how to handle pressure without passing it on. Someone who doesn't just dream of love, but builds a life stable enough to carry it.

Because love is not a vacation.
It's a *construction site.*
And I want to be ready.

Until then, I'll stay here. Watching. Learning.

And maybe preparing emotionally for the day I finally tell my parents, "So... I may be in love, and no, I promise he's not an internet scammer."

Fingers crossed. No fainting.

But beyond the giggles and ghosted WhatsApp texts, there's something that hits a bit deeper.

I see parents who used to dream big—now anxious, buried under responsibilities they can't even name anymore. They're supposed to be the 'grown-ups', but sometimes they look like tired teenagers who never got a chance to rest. It makes me wonder: is adulthood just youth with receipts?

And if it is, how come so many grown-ups look like they're being held together with half-done to-do lists and one remaining shred of hope?

I see kids with questions their parents can't answer—not because they don't care, but because they were never taught to ask themselves. It's like each generation inherits not just the surname, but the emotional glitches too.

What's wild is how we treat relationships like trophies—proof we're winning at life. But what if the real flex is knowing when not to enter one? Or walking away when love turns into a guilt trap wrapped in a good-morning text?

I’ve seen people get married just to escape loneliness, only to find it sitting next to them at the dinner table in a fancier outfit.

I’ve seen couples who post perfectly curated selfies but don’t even like each other when the filter’s off.

And let’s not even begin on how hard it is to tell your parents you're in love. The cultural acrobatics, the fear of judgment, the “log kya kahenge” background score playing in your head—it’s a full-time job. I just hope when my time comes, I don't need to file an RTI to have a simple heart-to-heart.

But here’s the thing I hold onto: maybe we’ll be the generation that breaks cycles, not bones. The ones who teach our kids emotional vocabulary before algebra. The ones who see love not as a rescue mission, but a choice—every single day.

And maybe, just maybe, when I look back at this chapter as an adult, I’ll smile and say, “Wow, you really thought you’d faint, huh?”

Spoiler: I probably will. But I’ll get up. With grace. And maybe a cookie.

CHAPTER-10

Chapter X: The Plot Twist I Didn't Order (But Got Anyway)

Spoiler Alert: Life doesn't care about your vision board. Especially not when you're 17 and everything suddenly feels like it's happening *at* you instead of *for* you.

Let me paint a picture for you: me, 17, mildly delusional with hope, slightly over-caffeinated, staring at the CBSE board results like I'm decoding alien hieroglyphics. Expected 95%, because you know, manifestation, hard work, late-night crying sessions with Physics. Got... less. Let's just say, less enough for me to want to throw my phone out the window and then jump after it.

And what did I do next?

Refreshed the page.

As if that would magically rewrite my marks. Spoiler: it didn't. I refreshed until CBSE's server probably thought I was launching a cyberattack. My brain? Fried. My heart? Cracked. My future? Question mark.

This was not the plot I wrote for myself. I had goals. I had dreams. I had pastel highlighters and a five-year plan written in cursive.

Phase One: Grief (Academic Edition)

I entered what I now call the Five Stages of Result Shock:

1. **Denial:**
"This can't be mine. Maybe there's another Daneet Kaur out there. Yes, must be a duplicate. CBSE, fix your database."
2. **Rage:**
"WHO CHECKED MY PAPER? I just wanna talk. Just a little conversation. With a sword."
3. **Bargaining:**
"If I start studying for my Bachelor's right now, maybe karma will reward me? Maybe I can fake a smile so convincingly, it becomes real?"

4. **Depression:**
"I'll just become a potato. Potatoes don't write exams. Potatoes don't cry. Potatoes are valid."
5. **Acceptance (reluctant):**
"Okay, so maybe I didn't get what I wanted. But maybe, just *maybe*, that's not the end of the world."

Phase Two: Existential Rethink

So here I was. 17. With a board result that felt like a slap. Sitting on a future that no longer fit. I started asking myself weirdly adult questions:

- Do I even *want* to study in India?
- Is the degree I chose something I love, or just something I felt I should do?
- What if I chose again? What if I tried again?

Here's what hit me: I wasn't stuck. I was just scared.

It wasn't that all doors were closed. I just didn't know where to knock.

Phase Three: The Unlikely Flame

Here comes the twist. A year ago, I dabbled in web designing. Just a school thing, an experiment, a try. But I liked it. The idea of building something from scratch. Something visual, functional, alive.

At the time, I didn't think much of it. But now, with my career dreams taking a nosedive thanks to a board result that felt like betrayal, I found myself circling back to that.

Then came Dad.

He saw me crumbling, and instead of giving me the classic "It's okay beta" speech, he tossed an idea: "What about Software Engineering?"

At first, I blinked.

Me? The almost-teacher? The one who always wanted to write lesson plans and stand in front of a class and say, "Open your notebooks" like I was the queen of knowledge?

Yes. That girl.

Because here's the thing: I still love teaching. But at that moment, it felt too far away. Too tied to a result that didn't reflect my effort. Too unfair.

So I looked at this new idea. A new path. A chance to rewrite my direction without rewriting who I am.

Phase Four: Dreaming Again (But Differently)

And then came the biggest decision: I want to go abroad for my Bachelor's.

Because honestly? Studying here felt... limiting. I want to be in classrooms where questions are welcomed, not shushed. Where assignments feel like explorations, not punishments. Where I can walk into a cafe, open my laptop, and *build* something.

And guess what? I started researching.

Right now, Australia is at the top of my list. It feels exciting — like a place where I could become someone entirely new. I've been looking up universities, exploring course structures, reading student reviews. I'm deep in YouTube rabbit holes watching "Day in the Life of a Software Engineering Student in Melbourne." I've even started prepping my paperwork.

My passport's ready. My hopes are packed. My eyes are set on that visa approval. Because if it doesn't come? I don't even want to think about that. Let's just say my backup plan is mild panic and probably ice cream.

But I believe it will. I have to.

Because this isn't just about a degree. It's about breathing again. It's about creating my own space, my own pace, and my own version of success.

Phase Five: Telling You This

Why am I writing this?

Because maybe you're 17 too. Maybe you also expected more. Maybe the world feels like it just slammed the door in your face and threw away the keys.

I want you to know something:

- You're not a number.

- You're not behind.
- You're not a failure.

You're just *beginning*.

If all your doors feel closed, build one. Out of code. Or poetry. Or rebellion. Or faith. But don't sit in the hallway forever.

Maybe you thought your life would look different by now. Maybe it still can.

Because plot twists don't mean the story's over. Sometimes, they mean it finally got interesting.

And me? I'm still learning, still healing, still hoping.

So if you're lost, come sit beside me. We'll refresh the page together.

Chapter X: The Plot Twist I Didn't Order (But Got Anyway)

Spoiler Alert: Life doesn't care about your vision board. Especially not when you're 17 and everything suddenly feels like it's happening *at* you instead of *for* you.

Let me paint a picture for you: me, 17, mildly delusional with hope, slightly over-caffeinated, staring at the CBSE board results like I'm decoding alien hieroglyphics. Expected 95%, because you know, manifestation, hard work, late-night crying sessions with Physics. Got... less. Let's just say, less enough for me to want to throw my phone out the window and then jump after it.

And what did I do next?

Refreshed the page.

As if that would magically rewrite my marks. Spoiler: it didn't. I refreshed until CBSE's server probably thought I was launching a cyberattack. My brain? Fried. My heart? Cracked. My future? Question mark.

This was not the plot I wrote for myself. I had goals. I had dreams. I had pastel highlighters and a five-year plan written in cursive.

Phase One: Grief (Academic Edition)

I entered what I now call the Five Stages of Result Shock:

1. **Denial:**

"This can't be mine. Maybe there's another Daneet Kaur out there. Yes, must be a duplicate. CBSE, fix your database."

2. **Rage:**

"WHO CHECKED MY PAPER? I just wanna talk. Just a little conversation. With a sword."

3. **Bargaining:**

"If I start studying for my Bachelor's right now, maybe karma will reward me? Maybe I can fake a smile so convincingly, it becomes real?"

4. **Depression:**

"I'll just become a potato. Potatoes don't write exams. Potatoes don't cry. Potatoes are valid."

5. **Acceptance (reluctant):**

"Okay, so maybe I didn't get what I wanted. But maybe, just *maybe*, that's not the end of the world."

Phase Two: Existential Rethink

So here I was. 17. With a board result that felt like a slap. Sitting on a future that no longer fit. I started asking myself weirdly adult questions:

- Do I even *want* to study in India?
- Is the degree I chose something I love, or just something I felt I should do?
- What if I chose again? What if I tried again?

Here's what hit me: I wasn't stuck. I was just scared.

It wasn't that all doors were closed. I just didn't know where to knock.

Phase Three: The Unlikely Flame

Here comes the twist. A year ago, I dabbled in web designing. Just a school thing, an experiment, a try. But I liked it. The idea of building something from scratch. Something visual, functional, alive.

At the time, I didn't think much of it. But now, with my career dreams taking a nosedive thanks to a board result that felt like betrayal, I found myself circling back to that.

Then came Dad.

He saw me crumbling, and instead of giving me the classic "It's okay beta" speech, he tossed an idea: "What about Software Engineering?"

At first, I blinked.

Me? The almost-teacher? The one who always wanted to write lesson plans and stand in front of a class and say, "Open your notebooks" like I was the queen of knowledge?

Yes. That girl.

Because here's the thing: I still love teaching. But at that moment, it felt too far away. Too tied to a result that didn't reflect my effort. Too unfair.

So I looked at this new idea. A new path. A chance to rewrite my direction without rewriting who I am.

Phase Four: Dreaming Again (But Differently)

And then came the biggest decision: I want to go abroad for my Bachelor's.

Because honestly? Studying here felt... limiting. I want to be in classrooms where questions are welcomed, not shushed. Where assignments feel like explorations, not punishments. Where I can walk into a cafe, open my laptop, and *build* something.

And guess what? I started researching.

Right now, Australia is at the top of my list. It feels exciting — like a place where I could become someone entirely new. I've been looking up universities, exploring course structures, reading student reviews. I'm deep in YouTube rabbit holes watching "Day in the Life of a Software Engineering Student in Melbourne." I've even started prepping my paperwork.

My passport's ready. My hopes are packed. My eyes are set on that visa approval. Because if it doesn't come? I don't even want to think about that. Let's just say my backup plan is mild panic and probably ice cream.

But I believe it will. I have to.

Because this isn't just about a degree. It's about breathing again. It's about creating my own space, my own pace, and my own version of success.

Phase Five: Telling You This

Why am I writing this?

Because maybe you're 17 too. Maybe you also expected more. Maybe the world feels like it just slammed the door in your face and threw away the keys.

I want you to know something:

- You're not a number.
- You're not behind.
- You're not a failure.

You're just *beginning.*

If all your doors feel closed, build one. Out of code. Or poetry. Or rebellion. Or faith. But don't sit in the hallway forever.

Maybe you thought your life would look different by now. Maybe it still can.

Because plot twists don't mean the story's over. Sometimes, they mean it finally got interesting.

And me? I'm still learning, still healing, still hoping.

So if you're lost, come sit beside me. We'll refresh the page together.

Epilogue: When the Detour Becomes the Road

There's something strange about walking down a path you never planned to take. The first few steps feel like betrayal — to the past version of you who dreamed differently. But then, slowly, the scenery starts to change. The air smells new. The road bends not into darkness, but into possibility.

Right now, I spend my days watching tutorials on coding logic and UX design. I'm planning my Statement of Purpose like it's the first letter to my future self. Every night, I check my email for any hint of that one golden ticket: the Australian offer letter.

It's terrifying. The what-ifs still scream sometimes. What if I don't get the visa? What if I'm not cut out for software engineering? What if I'm making the wrong choice... again?

But then I remember: I made it through the storm that tried to drown me. I walked through disappointment with grace (and a lot of snacks). I reimagined my future — not because I had to, but because I *chose to.*

That matters.

If the visa comes through, I'll step into a country I've never seen but already dream about. If it doesn't, I'll find another way. Because that's what we do — us plot-twist people. We pivot. We rewire. We get up again.

So to every 17-year-old sitting with uncertainty, to every person whose dream got delayed or denied — you're not a failure. You're just rewriting the blueprint.

And guess what?

The new one might just be better.

We're all works-in-progress. But doesn't that also mean we're full of potential?

Now, go. Not back to what was. But forward — to what *could be.*

Let's meet there.

With love and just enough sass,
Your Author

CHAPTER-11

This Isn't the End, It's the 'Ctrl+S' Moment

If you made it this far, congratulations. Either you really liked this book or you accidentally left it open while your phone died. Either way, I'm flattered. Let's wrap this rollercoaster up.

Here's the thing: life doesn't come with a user manual, a warranty, or a warning label that says, "Side effects may include confusion, heartbreak, existential dread, and also spontaneous dancing in your kitchen at 2 a.m."

We all start somewhere—maybe in a teenage bedroom filled with motivational sticky notes, or in a crowded bus with earbuds playing songs that feel like therapy. And we grow. Sometimes awkwardly. Sometimes dramatically. Sometimes slowly, like your download speed on a rainy day.

Adulthood, love, career, family, heartbreak, healing—it's all just messy. There's no fixed route. There's no "one right way." The best GPS in the world still says "recalculating" every time you take a detour. And spoiler: there will be *a lot* of detours.

But that's okay.

Because being lost isn't always a mistake. Sometimes it's how we find the *good stuff*. The stuff we didn't know we needed until we stumbled into it face-first. (Hopefully metaphorically. Unless you're clumsy. In which case, maybe literally.)

I wrote this book not as someone who has all the answers, but as someone who has all the questions—and the stubbornness to keep asking them.

You're allowed to question everything: your purpose, your path, your haircut. You're allowed to want big things and still feel small some days. You're allowed to cry about things that feel silly and laugh about things that aren't.

You're human.

And being human is wild. You're expected to pick a career at 17, fall in love with grace, make money, stay mentally healthy, maintain social connections, eat enough protein, and reply to emails—all while figuring out who you are and where your socks keep disappearing.

Sometimes, you'll wonder why you're the only one who doesn't have it figured out yet, while everyone else seems to be living a version of their life that's part success story, part carefully curated Instagram post. News flash: they don't have it figured out either. Most of them are just better at pretending, or they're looking at you and thinking, *Well, at least they have it together.*

But here's the magic trick: *nobody* has it all figured out. Not even your favorite celebrities or that person who always posts perfectly staged life updates. Behind the captions, they're probably crying over burnt toast and wondering if they chose the wrong font for their resume.

But that's the beauty of it all, isn't it? We're all here figuring it out together—albeit in different ways and at different speeds. And even though it's frustrating at times, it's also what makes life so wonderfully imperfect. If everything were perfect, would we even appreciate the moments that are? Think about it: what's a rainbow without a little rain?

But here's my unfiltered, unsolicited advice:

1. **Take breaks.** Mentally, emotionally, physically. Even Beyoncé rests.
2. **Find your people.** Not perfect ones—just honest ones. The ones who send you memes at 3 a.m. when you're having a crisis.
3. **Love without keeping score.** But also, keep your boundaries like a bouncer at a VIP club.
4. **Laugh often.** Especially at yourself. You're a walking sitcom.
5. **Don't let the world rush you.** Your timeline is yours. Not Instagram's. Not society's. Not your cousin who got married at 23 and now owns a house with two balconies.

And most importantly:

Write your story. In whatever font you want. With crossed-out words, messy margins, and doodles in the corner. Because your story—yes, *yours*—is worth telling. Even if it's not neat. Especially if it's not neat.

This isn't a goodbye.

This is a saved draft.

A warm hug in paragraph form.

An invisible fist bump from me to you.

Because you don't need to have everything figured out yet. And you don't need to be perfect. Just keep showing up, even when it feels like you're typing a novel that never seems to finish. Keep being messy, keep being bold, and most importantly, keep being you.

So go ahead. Keep growing. Keep unlearning. Keep choosing the kind of love, career, friendships, and version of yourself that feel real—not just impressive.

And when you fall—because you will—it's not the end. It's just your *Ctrl+S* moment. A pause. A save. A reminder that you're allowed to make mistakes, but you're also allowed to hit refresh and try again. Because sometimes, life's biggest breakthroughs come after we let go of the idea of having it all figured out.

The truth is? Nobody has it all figured out.

Some of us are just better at pretending.

And some of us write books instead.

Love,

Your (Not-So-Grown-Up) Author ♡

9 789334 305999